Jews at a Glance

JEWS
at a Glance

By

MAC DAVIS

Illustrated by

SAM NISENSON

HEBREW PUBLISHING COMPANY
New York

"I will insist that the Hebrews have done more to civilize men than any other nation. If I were an atheist and believed in blind eternal faith, I should still believe that fate had ordained the Jews to be the most essential instrument for civilizing the nations."

—JOHN ADAMS
Second President of the United States

You Will Meet

Some Words of Explanation About — My People

ANY BOOK of stories on the lives of the greatest Jews, the most famous, the most amazing, the most important, or the most extraordinary, is bound to be provocative and controversial. To write such a book takes a lot of research, a lot of work—and a lot of nerve.

However, again I have essayed this delicate but fascinating task, and here is the why of it.

Several years ago, I wrote my first book of biographies (*They All Are Jews*) which was well received. In that book were presented sixty Jews, from Moses to Einstein, who had left their mark upon civilization. Lack of space forced me to exclude from that gallery of greatness many eminent and interesting Jews.

"Do another book," urged my publisher, "but this time build a larger gallery of Jewish greatness and achievement." Hence, this book of biographies. Now, there are 114 Jews to meet.

This time, I have touched upon the lives of Jews before Moses and beyond Einstein. Literally, I have gone from A to Z—from Abraham, the father of all Hebrews to Adolph Zukor, the pioneer father of motion pictures.

Conscious that this is an age of speed and everything is done in a hurry, even reading, I offer in illustrated biographies of no more than two-minutes reading time for each, intimate companionship with 114 very unusual Jews who helped make our world what it was yesterday and what it is today.

My people were chosen from many places, from many fields of human endeavor, and from many periods of civilization. But all in this book are marked by the same two characteristics. All began as Jews, and all made things happen.

It was no easy task to select 114 unusual Jews from the many to be counted. While this selection represents the consensus of many who eagerly and most enthusiastically offered their opinions and knowledge, nevertheless, the responsibility for the final selection of these 114, is mine. Disagree with me if you will on the greatness or importance of some of the personalities chosen for this book, but none here are Jews to be ignored.

Some of my people were pioneers who created famous "firsts"—some shaped the history of the world—many improved the conditions under which everybody lives—some affected your modes of thought—some performed such epic achievements that they became the greatest in their fields, and some became the most famous and most unique in their. But all, without exception, have exerted some influence upon mankind.

In a stirring kaleidoscopic review, through the pages of this book, march the scientist, the inventor, the philosopher, the warrior, the patriot, the statesman, the artist, the actor, the playwright, the composer, the educator, the merchant, the philanthropist, the scholar, the rabbi, the singer, the jurist, the sports hero. It is a glowing collection of fascinating lives lived by towering Jewish figures of the past and present.

These biographies are intended for readers of all ages who have a lively curiosity about the lives and achievements of unusual Jews. Of course, a penetrating biography of an eminent and important figure cannot be written in a two-minute profile. Therefore, these lives-in-brief are not for the scholar. But such an amazing amount of general information and surprising fact have been crowded into all these stories, that even the most learned of readers may increase his knowledge of Jewish greatness and achievement by glancing through this book.

Perhaps these brief life stories will whet the interest of some readers and move them to search deeper into the history of the Jews who have achieved. Perhaps to others they will reveal the possibilities of greatness to which Jewish boys and girls may aspire. And perhaps other readers will find only excitement and pleasure to discover what makes great people tick. Whatever your reason for picking up this book, here are 114 very unusual Jews to know—with true stories of their lives, their deeds, and a brief evaluation of their influence upon the world.

These are my chosen people. I hope they also will be yours.

MAC DAVIS

Jews at a Glance

ABRAHAM

Father Of The Hebrews

In the land of the Chaldees lived a vain and wicked king named Nimrod who claimed to be himself a god. When the royal star-gazers told him that one would soon be born who would destroy the gods and take his crown, the wicked king decreed that all male infants be killed at birth to prevent this from happening.

In the city of Ur-Kuta, Entelai, wife of Terah, awaited the birth of her child. When Nimrod's decree became known, she fled to the desert and hid in a cave. There, in good time, a son was born to her. She named the infant Abraham. And when the baby hungered, an angel placed a stone in each of his little hands. From one stone flowed milk; from the other, honey.

For years, Abraham lived in the desert. He watched the sun and the moon and the stars in the heavens above him. And a great thought came to him as he contemplated the vastness of the universe. "There is One Who is the God of Gods and the Ruler of Rulers," he thought. "He is the One God who created heaven and earth."

Returning to Ur-Kuta with his mother, Abraham smashed his father's idols. The angry King Nimrod had him cast into a blazing furnace, but Abraham walked in the flames unscathed and unharmed. Frightened at this, the king begged Abraham to go away.

Abraham left his house and kinsmen, and traveled up and down the land, preaching against idols wherever he went. He passed through many dangers, witnessing the destruction of the evil cities of Sodom and Gomorrah. He waged war with a handful of men against five mighty kings to rescue his nephew, Lot. And he became the father of two great nations. One, through the son of his wife Hagar, founded the Ishmaelites. The other, through the son of his wife Sarah, founded the nation of the Israelites.

So faithful to God was Abraham that he unwaveringly placed his own beloved son on the sacrificial altar in obedience to His command. And it is told that he lived to the great age of 175 years, and all his days were full of wondrous events.

The son of Terah was the first man to come to believe in One God when all others on earth still worshipped idols. And it is for this great concept that Abraham is most worthy to be remembered.

Jacob
ADLER

All The World Was His Stage

To Jacob Adler belongs the distinction of having been the greatest and most famous Yiddish actor of all time. For fifty years he held audiences all over the world enthralled by the power and sweep of his performances. No actor did more to raise the cultural level of the Yiddish theatre. Nor was his own acting the sole contribution he made to the stage. At one time or another, there were seven Adlers performing somewhere in the theatre or movies.

Born in Odessa in 1855, Adler was discovered in an amateur group by the great Yiddish dramatist, Abraham Goldfadden. Adler left Russia in 1882 to escape the Czarist persecutions and emigrated to America. In a short time, after some difficulties, he became the greatest and most popular actor on the Yiddish stage. His work was an inspiration to a rising group of young Yiddish playwrights.

Jacob Adler brought his art to every Yiddish-speaking community in the world. He played every kind of role imaginable, even playing Shylock in Yiddish with an English-speaking company. His "King Lear" in English was one of the theatre's most memorable performances.

So fabulous a legend did he become that even at 70 people clamored for him to return to the stage for a last time. On the opening night of his farewell appearance, the old Adler, semi-paralyzed, almost voiceless and deaf, could not hear the knocking on his dressing room door that called him to the stage for his first entrance. But it was so loud that all the audience packed breathlessly in their seats could hear it clearly. They rose in their places. "Adler koomt!" they shouted. Their cry echoed in the street outside where thousands who had been unable to get into the theatre took up the shout of "Adler koomt! Adler koomt!"

In the theatre, at last, the old man, leaning heavily on a cane, came stumbling on stage. The audience burst into tears at the sight of this hollow shell of a man. His voice did not carry over the footlights but no one protested. When Adler left the stage, many again wept for the sick old man.

A year later, Jacob Adler died. More than a quarter of a million mourners went to his funeral and wept for the great and beloved Yiddish actor.

Sholom ALEICHEM

He Made The World Laugh

The Jews have ever been noted for finding humor in their bitter misery. Spokesmen for all of them, and the greatest humorist the Jewish people has ever produced, was the beloved short story writer, poet, playwright and novelist, Sholom Aleichem.

Sholom Aleichem, born Solomon Rabinowitz, was the son of a rabbi in Pereyeslav, Ukrainia. Even as a small boy, he loved to poke fun at the many pompous and self-important people who came to call on his father. He was often punished for his mockery, but there was rarely any unkindness in what he did. For it was one of the basic characteristics of his attitude to his own people all his life that even when he laughed at them he loved them with all his heart.

When his father became poor, the boy studied to be a teacher. He became a rabbi and gave lessons for a living, but soon he was putting down on paper his impressions of the poor and miserable Jews with whom he came in constant contact. Stories, poems, plays poured from his versatile pen. He wrote in Yiddish, the common language of the Eastern European Jew, and published his work under the pseudonym of "Sholom Aleichem," a Hebrew phrase which means literally, "Peace be with you," but which is normally used as a phrase of greeting among Jews.

His writings reached the hearts of all who read them. He was translated into all languages, and so universal were his ideas, so true and meaningful his humor, that anyone, no matter what the language, could understand and appreciate Sholom Aleichem and the world he wrote about.

In 1905, he came to America to escape the frightful persecution of the Jews in Russia. After living in New York for a few years, he returned briefly to Russia, only to return to the United States at the outbreak of World War I. Depressed and shaken by the death of his son and the misery of the Jewish people in war-torn Europe, the great humorist died in 1916 and was buried in Brooklyn. But, though he is no longer among us, Sholom Aleichem still has his eager and laughing audience wherever in all the world there are Jews who read the Yiddish language.

Mel ALLEN

A Mouthpiece for Sports

Probably no man in history, however important as he may have been in his time, was ever listened to by as many people as have heard the voice of Mel Allen. His rich, warm and distinctive voice broadcasting on radio and television the details of some sports event, like a daily baseball game, a world series, or a Rose Bowl football classic, has been heard in any one year, by more than two-hundred million people.

America's most popular sportscaster was born as Melvin Allen Israel, in Birmingham, Alabama, in 1913. He was the son of Russian immigrants. His father owned a general store. Although, he graduated from high school at the age of 15, young Mel was no bookworm but an active American lad who starred in football, baseball and basketball. He even served a minor league baseball team as a bat boy.

At the University of Alabama, he was a sports writer for the campus newspaper. After earning his degree in 1932, he went on to study law and win his degree in 1936. As a student, he worked in a shoe store and held a fellowship under which he taught speech at the University. It led to his appointment as manager of the campus public address system. It was almost inevitable that he go on from that to broadcasting sports.

One day, while announcing a football game over a local radio station, his rich Southern voice attracted the attention of an important executive of the Columbia Broadcasting System. The executive persuaded him to abandon his career as a lawyer, come to New York, and become a sports commentator for the network. At the same time, Melvin Allen Israel was persuaded to change his name to Mel Allen—for public identification.

By 1941, the little-known Mel Allen had become so popular as a sports announcer that his salary zoomed to $35,000 a year. Two years later, he became the radio voice of the New York Yankees.

Through the years, he won many honors as a sports commentator. In 1950, his popularity reached such heights of public devotion, that he was given a "Mel Allen Day" in the vast Yankee Stadium, as if he were one of the most famous of baseball stars. He received thousands of dollars in cash gifts from his many devoted and adoring listening fans. He turned the money over to a university to be distributed in scholarships for needy boys. The honor of the occasion was richly deserved. Mel Allen had become not only the highest-paid sports voice in America, with an annual income in six figures, but he also became the most popular and the most famous sports announcer in the world.

David
BELASCO

Maker Of Stage Miracles

A man of eccentric manner both in dress and demeanor, David Belasco was nonetheless one of the greatest influences on the American theatre. When he first appeared in New York as a young director and author, the theatre was relatively cheap and tawdry, as well as unnatural and unrealistic. Belasco breathed new life into an old art, and brought naturalism and the modern touch to the stage. He made actors out of ordinary performers and great actresses out of simple and untrained girls.

At the same time, Belasco was contributing many significant features to the theatre itself. He was the first to introduce electric lighting to the stage as well as altering its very appearance. What he did to the style and manner of the performer was practically a revolution in the art of acting. No one could ever mistake a Belasco production since it was indelibly stamped with his own inimitable touch and genius.

David Belasco, son of a leading English comic actor, was born in San Francisco in 1853. His father, an orthodox Jew, had gone there to prospect for gold. At 16, young David was through with school and trying his hand at show business. For several years he trouped from town to town as actor, manager, playwright.

Since his short stature and high-pitched voice were handicaps in his acting, Belasco soon turned exclusively to directing, producing and writing for the stage. When work out West ran low, he came East to tackle the New York stage. Soon he became famous as a director. In that role, he was noted as harsh, dictatorial, autocratic, but above all imaginative. People flocked to his plays as his fame grew. The finest actors and actresses in the world clamored to work for him. Before his career ended, he had produced over 400 plays, including some 150 he had written himself. He had built his own theatre after his own design which is still in existence and still bears his name. He had produced plays in Europe as well as America, and he became a legend in the theatre long before he passed away.

Little of his fame remains today, other than the theatre that bears his name. Yet David Belasco's influence is plain to see in almost every play shown. The American theatre can truly thank him for raising it to an artistic level as high as any in the world.

David Ben- GURION

Little Giant Of Israel

A short, powerfully-built man with bright blue eyes and a halo of white hair, the figure of David Ben-Gurion strides through history, a giant in miniature, a leader of the Jewish people fit to stand level with their ancient Biblical heroes. Ben-Gurion proved, as the first Prime Minister of Israel, that under certain circumstances, a man can be indispensable. Without his strong arm at the helm, it is hard to say what might have happened in the trying years of Israel's painful rebirth.

Ben-Gurion, born David Green in Poland, grew up in an atmosphere of Zionism and was already a leader presiding over Zionist meetings before he was 14. Jailed by the authorities for his activities, he left for Palestine to continue the struggle. He worked as a farmer, rising quickly to a place of leadership. When World War I broke out, the Turkish government exiled him from Palestine because of his vigorous support of the Allies from whom he expected help for the Zionist cause.

He came to America and there helped organize an American branch of the Jewish Legion. When the electrifying news of the Balfour Declaration came out, Ben-Gurion left for England to join the British Army. He was then 31.

After World War I, he returned to Palestine to carry on the struggle. He founded Histadrut, Israel's giant labor federation now so vital in the development of the country. He fought to create a Jewish Army and denounced moderation and patience as advocated by others for the realization of a Jewish homeland.

On May 14, 1948, 62-year-old David Ben-Gurion announced to the world that Israel was at last a living nation. His lifetime dream had at last come true. In the war against the Arabs that followed, he was the strong man who created the army that beat back the savage attack and forced the enemy to make peace. He was elected Israel's first Prime Minister and Minister of Defense in the first general election in 1949. In 1953, he lay down his burden of office to take up life again as a simple farmer. But the danger of a new war brought him back into his country's leadership, and in 1956, the little giant was again at the helm as Israel's strong man and Prime Minister.

Judah Philip BENJAMIN

Rebel For A Lost Cause

An honored member of the cabinet of Jefferson Davis during the Civil War, Judah P. Benjamin served, in turn, as Attorney-General, Secretary of War, and Secretary of State for the Confederated States of America. So heavily did President Davis lean on the little giant from New Orleans in all matters that he came to be known as "the brains of the Confederacy." No Jew in America had ever held so high a post in government before.

Judah P. Benjamin was born in the West Indies and came to Charleston as a boy. He entered Yale at 15, and the brilliant youngster began to teach English in New Orleans a couple of years later. He became a highly successful lawyer in the South he loved, and rose to the top of his profession. When he was warned of failing eyesight, he gave up the practice of law and established a sugar plantation with great success. Floods swept away his fortune and he was obliged to resume the law. Before long, he rose to prominence in politics. From the State Legislature, he went on to the United States Senate at the age of 48, second of his people to attain that high office.

When the Civil War broke out and Louisiana withdrew from the Union, Benjamin resigned his seat in the U.S. Senate to join the cabinet of Jefferson Davis. Proud of being a Jew, he withstood many personal attacks on him because of his faith, and worked prodigiously for the Southern cause until Lee's surrender to Grant at Appomattox. Then Benjamin, past fifty years of age, fled to escape hanging. Penniless and a fugitive, he made his way to England. There he started anew when life must have seemed hopeless. But he was admitted to the English bar after six months of study. He again became prominent as a lawyer. He received signal honors from many of Britain's greats, and amassed a large fortune. With it all, Judah P. Benjamin's thoughts ever turned to his beloved land. When he died, in 1884, he was rich and full of honors, but he still longed for his home in America. Though he never returned, two of his homes—one in Louisiana and another in Florida—were converted into historic shrines in memory of the little man who had devoted his life to a lost cause.

[21]

Sarah BERNHARDT

The Divine Sarah

Daughter of a brief union between a lawyer and a Paris milliner, both Dutch Jews, this thin, sickly child was handed over to a nurse to be raised and promptly forgotten by her mother. Until she was 5, the slums of Paris were her home, and dirt and poverty her every-day companions. She scrubbed floors, ate scraps, learned nothing but the unsavory language and manners of the back alleys. Living in a dark and ill-smelling room, little Sarah was close to tuberculosis when she met an aunt one day and begged to be taken from her surroundings. Her plea was ignored. Little Sarah threw herself from a window, injuring herself severely.

A few days later, her mother appeared on the scene. Sarah was taken away for two years during which she was an invalid. At 7, her mother sent her to a boarding school. She could not read or write, and was so bashful that everyone considered her to be stupid.

At the school, Sarah was a trial to her teachers. She was wild, mischievous and un-loved. At 15, she was offered a chance to go to the conservatory to study acting. Screaming with rage, she refused. Her mother threatened to send her back to the slums. Sarah went to the conservatory.

At 17, Sarah finished her acting studies. She had distinguished herself at the school and she was promptly hired by the Comédie Française, most distinguished theatre in Europe.

Her first appearance was a dismal failure. The critical notices were bad. Heartbroken, Sarah took poison. For several days, her life hung on a thread, then she recovered.

At the Comédie, Sarah was the same un-tamed, wild-tempered girl she had always been. She was forced to resign after a fight with another actress. She took to wandering around Europe. Then, a few years later, at 22, Sarah decided she would learn acting.

Now, with passion, she dedicated herself to the theatre. In two years, she soared to the summit as the world's greatest actress. A thousand legends sprang up around her. Always, behind them, was the sure magic of her art. She became the Divine Sarah.

At 71, she lost a leg by amputation. In spite of it, she continued to work in the theatre. She died at 79, while making a film. Camille had been her greatest role. But her own life had been her greatest play.

Irving BERLIN

He Wrote The Songs For A Nation To Sing

Irving Berlin rose from the sidewalks of New York and the deepest poverty to become the world's most famous writer of popular songs. Truly has it been said that this dark little man wrote the songs of America. No one has affected popular music more than he, nor written more songs that have received great popular approval. Literally thousands of songs have poured from his fertile imagination. And yet, Irving Berlin knew practically nothing about the technical aspects of music. He never had any musical education. As a matter of fact, his entire education consisted of two years of schooling as a child.

Irving Berlin was born in Siberia in 1888 as Israel Baline. When his parents were forced to flee their home after a pogrom, little Izzy was brought to America at the age of 4. His father, who was a cantor in his spare time, died when the boy was barely 8 years old. And from the time he was 14, the boy was on his own.

He sold newspapers on the streets, and earned pennies leading a blind singer through the streets of the Bowery. Later he became a singing waiter in low dives and saloons. And finally he wrote his first song. It was "Marie from Sunny Italy," and it brought him the measly pittance of 37 cents in earnings.

But it was the beginning, and Irving Berlin went on to earn millions from the songs that followed steadily afterwards. With the publication of "Alexander's Ragtime Band," he became famous. Not only was it his first hit song, but it has remained one of the best-known songs he ever wrote. Among the songs which have done so much to endear him to people all over the world are, "Easter Parade," "White Christmas," and "God Bless America," which has become accepted as much of a national anthem as is "The Star Spangled Banner."

Irving Berlin reaped another fortune with phenomenal success in the theatre and in musical motion pictures. For nearly four decades, Irving Berlin remained the acknowledged master of popular music, and in 1956, song hits were still coming from his ever-lively imagination for a nation to sing. Many of the songs he has written will live on as long as America loves to sing a song.

[23]

Emil
BERLINER

A Most Useful American Citizen

Born in Germany in 1851, Emil Berliner came to the United States when he was 19. Penniless when he landed at Ellis Island, he went to work as a bottle-washer, earning $6 a week. At night, he attended free classes at famed Cooper Union in New York, and passed up meals so he could scrape together enough pennies to buy second-hand books on scientific subjects.

At 26, his privations and hard study saw their first fruit when he invented the telephone transmitter. Although he was the first man to do so, he was so poor that he was unable to hire a lawyer to obtain the necessary patent for this important invention that was to make commercial telephony possible. It took 14 years of waiting for the Supreme Court of the United States to decree that Berliner was entirely justified in his contention that his invention had been made prior to that of Thomas Edison.

In 1888, Berliner predicted in a lecture that the time would come when singers and speakers would be able to make their voices heard around the world. He himself did much to make this dream come true by his invention of the microphone that made radio broadcasting possible, as well as improvements on the gramophone and phonograph. He invented the stylus which records sound and the method of duplicating disc records. In 1917, he invented the air-cooled engine with revolving cylinder now used extensively in airplanes.

While best known as the inventor of the first talking machine, Berliner was also responsible for making the helicopter a workable flying machine. His son in 1919 actually flew in Berliner's helicopter.

Among other inventions made by Emil Berliner was an acoustic tile that improved the acoustic properties of many buildings. And his work on microphones and transmitters made the motion picture projector possible.

When the great inventor died, President of the United States Herbert Hoover said of him, "Emil Berliner was one of America's most useful citizens."

Leonard
BERNSTEIN

Young Man Of Many Music Affairs

On November 14, 1943, a virtually unknown young man of 25 was suddenly called upon to conduct the great New York Philharmonic Symphony Orchestra. The next day, newspapers across the country carried front page stories of the young man's tremendous triumph in the most difficult task a musician can be called on to undertake. Some papers even carried editorials. No more dramatic or successful debut had ever been made by a conductor.

Some said that young Leonard Bernstein was too flamboyant on the podium. They claimed he was egocentric, more so than even a conductor had a right to be. But they agreed that he had a consummate mastery over the orchestra, the score, and the audience. And they agreed that, above all else, Leonard Bernstein was the greatest baton discovery of the last several decades.

The young man went on to repeat his triumph many times. He appeared as guest conductor with most major American orchestras. Wherever he conducted, here or abroad, he received ovation after ovation for his brilliant leadership. In Palestine, he received the greatest ovation an American conductor ever received anywhere.

Nevertheless, the ever-increasing fame of Leonard Bernstein does not rest on his achievements as a conductor alone. He is truly a genius of many affairs. As a composer, he has conquered not one, but all fields of music. In symphonic music, he has impressed with his "Jeremiah Symphony." He has written an impressive jazz symphony. For ballet, he composed the scintillating scores of "Fancy Free" and "Facsimile." He has written tuneful scores for "On the Town," a musical comedy smash, and others. And there was his stirring music for other musical comedies which were fantastically successful as Broadway hit shows. And there was the stirring music for the prize-winning motion picture, "On The Waterfront."

He is also a remarkably endowed pianist who can play Mozart or boogie-woogie with equal facility. Hollywood saw his handsome profile, and yearned to make him a screen star, but Bernstein has refused fabulous offers from Hollywood. He has become a celebrated music teacher.

This unusual young man of many feverish activities was born in Lawrence, Massachusetts, on August 25, 1918. Music has been his life from the beginning. When he was 19, a world-famous conductor urged him to change his name for he warned him that a name like "Bernstein" would prove too great an obstacle to success. But Leonard Bernstein refused to search for his place in the world under a false name. And the world is infinitely richer for his dedication to his art as a brilliant conductor, a composer of serious works, musical comedies, ballets, modern jazz and opera, and teaching.

Hayyim Nahman BIALIK

Immortal Hebrew Poet

Foremost Hebrew poet of his time, Chaim Nachman Bialik was the son of an incredibly poor but learned scholar in a tiny Russian village. So poor were the Bialiks that even the family candlesticks had to be pawned to buy bread. And when the boy's father, a broken-hearted dreamer, died when his son was only 7, Mrs. Bialik went to work as a peddler to support her son. She toiled from dawn to midnight, and the memory of that time of poverty and privation left its mark on the sensitive child and colored most of the great poetry he wrote in later years.

The bitterness of his own life filled him with sympathy for the harsh lives of his people too. When he was sent to live with his pious but strict grandfather, the boy began to show signs of an unusually brilliant mind. At the age of 11, he had already read many of the great works of the Talmud. At 18, he went to live in Odessa. His first poem, and one of his greatest, was called "El-Ha-Zipor," and astounded the liter-ary world when at last it was permitted to see the light of day. For six months the timid young man had carried it crumpled in his pocket, afraid to show it to anyone.

Bialik wrote more and more poetry in Hebrew, taught school, and grew in stature as the voice of his people and their longing for a homeland. In 1923, Bialik at last moved to Palestine where he lived till his death in 1934.

Long before death overtook the Hebrew poet, he had become a living legend to the Jewish people. A master of Hebrew prose as well as poetry, he had endeared himself to all who knew him. He wrote many marvelous sketches of Jewish life and fascinating tales for children based on Biblical themes.

Beloved by all Jews, Bialik left behind imperishable memories of himself as a sweet-natured and kindly man. His home, on Bialik Street in Tel Aviv, has become a cultural museum and national shrine. In it are lovingly displayed many of his manuscripts and poems. But his shrine is as much in the hearts of his people as in the mementoes he left behind.

Franz
BOAS

He Exploded The Racial Theory

Of all the great scientists of history, none has had a more profound influence on modern thought and understanding than Franz Boas. A student of human life, Boas upset many old ideas about mankind. Anthropology, the study of man, was his field of activity, and some of his findings in that field are of basic importance in modern knowledge. Boas showed that there was no fundamental difference in the way primitive and civilized man think, that there is no inborn difference between Negro and white, that there are no superior or inferior races of mankind. And he believed with his whole heart that the suppression of intellectual freedom would destroy science altogether.

The author of these revolutionary concepts was born in Germany in 1858, the son of a merchant in comfortable circumstances. After his university studies, Boas set out, at 25, on his first expedition, to Baffinland to study the Eskimo. In 1884, when German intellectual life began to stifle him, he came to America. After a second field trip to the Pacific Northwest, he accepted an appointment as Professor of Anthropology at Columbia in 1899. Two years later, he also became Curator of Anthropology at the American Museum of Natural History.

Boas organized many important expeditions in order to establish the truth of his theories, and set up a series of studies for the government in relation to child guidance and welfare. In 1905, he left the Museum to concentrate on his teaching. It was then that he began to develop the small group of students and associates who were to make over anthropology into what it has since become. Meanwhile, he investigated the nature of aging and the problems of language, becoming in the process a self-made linguist.

Franz Boas remained as professor at Columbia for nearly 50 years, retiring in 1937 at 79. Needless to say, he lived through the burning of his books by the infamous Hitler, who found unbearable the findings by Franz Boas that there was no such thing as a superior race. It was while expounding this fact at a luncheon in 1942 that the great student of mankind suddenly died.

Louis D. BRANDEIS

The First Judge For The Supreme Court

It was in the year 1916 that President Woodrow Wilson made the precedent-breaking appointment that saw the first Jew in history named as a member of the United States Supreme Court. The choice could have fallen on no better man than Louis Brandeis, already famed in the land for his humanitarianism, his knowledge of the law, and his tireless work for freedom.

The naming of Brandeis was met with a storm of protest and an outburst of cheers. The protests came from the powerful interests who had smarted under the attacks made on them by the famous lawyer. They called him radical and Jew. The cheers came from the humble and the weak, the oppressed and the needy, all who had been helped and supported by Louis Brandeis, champion of the underprivileged and defender of the people's rights.

In answer to those who protested, President Wilson had only this to say: "Brandeis is a friend of justice and of men." A still better answer came in the 22 years of distinguished service he was to give on the highest court of the land. When, at 85, Brandeis stepped down from his seat on the bench, the whole nation acclaimed him with a single voice.

The son of Bohemian immigrants, Louis Brandeis was born in Louisville, Kentucky. He attended Harvard Law School and, at 21, set up his little office for the practice of law in Boston. In a few years, he had reached national prominence as an advocate. In spite of his great earnings, he was noted far and wide for his integrity and for his willingness to take any case he believed in. He earned the name of "People's Advocate" by his stubborn fight to help the lowly, the poor and the downtrodden.

He became famous for his defence of labor unions and human rights. Active in Zionist affairs, he worked to the end of his life for the restoration of the ancient homeland. And when he died, in 1941, it was with the knowledge that the workers of Palestine, out of love and respect for the great jurist, had established a colony in his honor and called it Ain-Ha-Shofet—The Well of the Judge.

Eddie
CANTOR

Beloved Comedian

One of the longest and most glorious careers in show business belongs to the beloved Eddie Cantor, most widely known of theatre personalities. In every medium, stage, screen, radio and television, he has delighted and amused millions of people since he first made his appearance as a singing waiter in Coney Island way back in 1910.

Born in New York on the lower East Side in 1892, Cantor came from the usual poverty-stricken background of most immigrant families. Attracted to the theatre, he early joined the fabulous Gus Edwards kid revue along with George Jessel and Walter Winchell.

When he became a celebrated star with the Ziegfeld Follies, Eddie Cantor's distinctive style of comedy and singing made him the most popular entertainer in the land. But the pop-eyed star never forgot the underprivileged background from which he himself had sprung. He financed a camp for poor children, and raised funds for Youth Aliyah to help refugee youngsters escape Hitler. He appeared in hundreds of benefits for worthy causes, giving unstintingly of his time and talent wherever sought.

With all the joy he has brought audiences, and all the fine work he did for the underprivileged and oppressed, no deed of Eddie Cantor's is more outstanding than what he did in the struggle against the terrible killer, polio. Not only did he originate the famous "March of Dimes," but he gave that nation-wide campaign its name.

Begun by him in 1936, the March of Dimes became one of the widest spread and best known campaigns against disease. Thousands of children and grown-ups too can be grateful for what it accomplished. It was for his work for the March of Dimes as much as for his eminence as an actor and philanthropist in other fields that Temple University in 1951 awarded Eddie Cantor the honorary degree of Doctor of Humane Letters. It was the first time an American actor was honored with such an award. For his humanitarian work he also was cited by the Congress of the United States.

As president of the Jewish Theatrical Guild, as philanthropist, as originator of a great humanitarian campaign, as an actor and a comedian, Eddie Cantor richly deserves the praise of his own people and the love of all Americans. Hollywood itself placed its stamp of approval on a famous and universally-loved human being when it made the motion picture known as "The Eddie Cantor Story."

Al CAPP

A Comic Strip Artist

One of the important phenomena of American journalism is the comic strip that appears in practically every newspaper in the land. Millions of people turn to them even before looking at the headlines. They have made their readers laugh, cry and think. And their influence has grown to astounding proportions.

Most popular and most widely read of the men who create comic strips is Al Capp, inventor of "Li'l Abner." Born in New Haven, Connecticut, in 1909, as Alfred Caplin, he was drawing and selling his own comics strip to neighborhood children before he was 11. A year later, a great tragedy overtook him when, in a street car accident, he lost his right leg. Nevertheless, young Al Capp went on to high school and then art school. In spite of his handicap, he even worked at odd jobs to earn art school fees.

When Al Capp was 23, the Associated Press hired him to draw the pictures for an already established strip. He became, thereby, the nation's youngest cartoonist, though quite un-known. But he lost this unique distinction when he soon was fired.

Persisting in his ambition, Al became a 'ghost artist' for various cartoonists, working at one time on three different comic strips but remaining always in the background and anonymous. It was not until 1934 that he essayed the preparation of his own comic strip. His new creation was called Li'l Abner and it appeared for the first time in only 8 newspapers. The strip dealt with the amusing and fantastic antics of a character named Abner Yokum and his hillbilly family and friends.

Li'l Abner became a fabulous success. By 1947, it was appearing in 500 newspapers with a daily reading public of more than 30 million people. Even a motion picture was made, based on the popular and successful comic strip.

Li'l Abner has proved to be more than just another comic strip. In it Al Capp has written friendly satire on people, customs and events in American life. It has brought Al Capp national fame and fortune. More than that, Li'l Abner has made him famous as the world's greatest contemporary comic strip artist.

Emanuel CELLER

Congressman From Brooklyn

Since the beginning of American government, many Jews have been elected to the Congress of the United States. Of them all, Emanuel Celler has served longer than any Jew in history. In 1956, Celler was completing his 34th consecutive year as a Representative in the United States Congress.

Son of a wine merchant, Emanuel Celler was born in Brooklyn, New York, in 1888. When his parents died soon after he entered Columbia, Celler became head of his household with a number of orphaned brothers and sisters to support. He went to work as a wine salesman, meanwhile continuing his studies at night. He graduated from Columbia in 1910, and two years later was admitted to the bar.

His first legal fee was $25. He established a fine reputation among the poor and underprivileged by his work on their behalf. When he was offered the Democratic nomination for Congress from the then 10th Congressional District, Celler eagerly accepted. He did not know that others before him had declined the nomination because it was thought a Democrat could not win in that strong Republican district. But it did not matter. Celler entered the campaign with vim and zest. He enlisted the help of his friends and relatives, made speeches on every street corner. The result was a big political upset. Celler was elected to Congress by some 3,000 votes.

From his first term in Congress, Celler began to work for reform and social betterment. Each time he returned to Brooklyn at election time, his plurality grew larger than the time before. First sent to Washington in 1922, he was never thereafter beaten. In 1952, his margin of victory, once a mere 3,000 votes, had risen to over 90,000.

With the passage of years, Emanuel Celler won a deserved reputation as a fighter in Congress, often on the side of unpopular causes, always on the side of the little man. He fought for liberal immigration, for civil rights and against discrimination. He made many impassioned appeals, to the White House and other places, for support of Israel and the Jewish homeland. As Chairman of the powerful House Judiciary Committee, Emanuel Celler was, in 1956, still in the thick of the fight, one of America's great liberals who had held his seat in Congress longer than any other Jew in American history.

Marc
CHAGALL

Painter Of The Jewish Soul

As a child in Vitebsk, Russia, Marc Chagall loved nothing better than to sit in the yard behind his house munching bread and butter and looking at everything around him. He observed the people who went by, the sky, the earth. When he went to the *cheder* where he was taught, and to the synagogue, he again spent much of his time watching the men in their prayer shawls, the holy shrine, the pulpit, the chandeliers. Whatever he looked at left a deep impression on him, never to be forgotten in the years that were to come.

His father, a poor worker in a herring store, hoped that the boy would grow up to be a rabbi. Marc went to Hebrew schools until he was 16. His mother wasn't satisfied with the narrow education her son was getting and wanted him to acquire secular knowledge as well. Meantime, young Marc had discovered that it was fun to draw. And he lost his taste for study as he grew fonder of drawing pictures.

One day, young Marc persuaded his mother to take him to an art teacher. She was at first horrified by the idea, but reluctantly gave in. Marc went to study art and his father, who was furious, grudgingly paid out the five rubles that were the monthly fee.

In three months Marc discovered that he knew more than his teacher. With a few rubles in his pocket, he set out for St. Petersburg and a better art school. He took a job as a servant to get along while studying. Three years later, he was back in Vitebsk. There he painted pictures of his own town, pictures with a soul, a Jewish soul. He portrayed the Jews, their sorrows, their joys.

When he was 21, a wealthy Jewish lawyer gave him a monthly allowance to help him keep body and soul together. He went to Paris to continue his studies. His painting began to show a new power and style. But always he clung to the subject matter he knew best: the town of Vitebsk and its people, the Jewish life that was so deeply and completely his own. And surely there came to Marc Chagall recognition as the greatest lyric painter in the world, a master of brilliant color and craftsmanship.

Morris
Raphael
COHEN

A Man From Minsk

Morris Raphael Cohen was one of America's greatest teachers and one of the great philosophers of the 20th century. A man who sought truth all his life, Cohen trained hundreds of students to become thinkers instead of disciples.

Born in Minsk in 1880, he was a sickly child. His early years were passed in extreme poverty. He spent many hours in cheder, often going barefoot to school with only a chunk of black bread for his day's food. He became an avid reader, of secular Yiddish literature as well as of the Talmud.

At 12, his mother brought him to America to join his father who had preceded them. In spite of continued poverty, young Morris proved a brilliant student in the public schools. He entered City College of New York at 15 and that place of learning was to become his major interest for the rest of his life.

It was not until 1902, after poor success as a public school teacher, that Cohen received an appointment at City College to teach algebra and geometry. A fellowship gave him the chance to go to Harvard where he earned his Ph.D. In 1906, he returned to City College. He asked to be allowed to teach philosophy instead of mathematics but was turned down. Nor would any

other university take him on as a teacher of philosophy.

Haunted by a feeling of failure, he took up the study of law, though his hopes still lay in his beloved philosophy. At last, in 1912, his fondest dream was realized when City College offered him a post as Assistant Professor of Philosophy. He threw himself into the new job with all his heart and soul. His brilliant teaching and his passion for philosophy kindled sparks inside his students, many of whom went on to distinguished careers as rabbis, ministers of Christianity, celebrated judges, and prominent citizens in public life.

In 1938, City College's most celebrated professor who had become an almost legendary figure in American philosophy and education, retired. He had been at the institution for 43 years, both as a student and teacher. Scores of articles and books had come from his pen to express his philosophy and influence American life. In one place, he had written: "Brief is the life of man and of uncertain duration is his handiwork. But the echoes from soul to soul will go on so long as human life lasts." Morris Cohen must have meant that about himself, for his mind and memory as one of the greatest philosophers of the 20th century still live in American thought.

DAVID

Sweet Singer Of Songs

Of all the children of Jesse, the weaver, and his wife, Nazbat, none was more beautiful, more graceful and slender and swift of foot, than the youngest who was called David, which means beloved. As a young boy, David tended his father's sheep. And as he did so, he played endlessly on his kinnor, which was a little harp with ten strings, and sang little songs like prayers that he made up himself. David was a fearless shepherd and he tended his father's flock well.

One day, a prophet came to tell Jesse that his son, David, had been chosen to become King of Israel when Saul's days were ended. Jesse sent the boy to bring food to his three brothers who were in the army of King Saul and downcast in the shadow of defeat by the Philistines. For Goliath, a great giant warrior nearly ten feet tall, was challenging Saul to send out someone against him to determine in single combat the outcome of the entire war.

David volunteered to face the giant, Goliath. "The Lord is my shield," he said to King Saul. "I do not fear ten Goliaths." And, in the valley between the camps of the two armies,

David at last was permitted to face the Philistine giant. All he carried was a shepherd's sling and a shepherd's pouch. As David drew near to the giant, he drew from his pouch a smooth stone and fitted it to the sling. And he flung the stone at Goliath and pierced the giant's forehead, tumbling him into the dust. And then, with Goliath's own sword, he cut off the Philistine's head.

David won the gratitude of his people by his conquest, and when King Saul died, he became king and reigned over his people for forty years. He united the Jewish kingdom, won Jerusalem, and planned the building of the Temple. But his greatest fame was won as a great musician and a sweet singer. He wrote the Psalms, most beautiful of songs, and praised the Lord all the days of his life. And when, as King, he did one of his soldiers a great wrong, he wept with shame and sorrow for the sin he had done. And he lived thereafter a life of righteousness, singing always his love of God and ruling his people with strength and wisdom. Weary at last of many wars, and old in years, he called in his son, Solomon, and made him King in his place.

Jo DAVIDSON

Thinker In Bronze—Poet In Clay

It was almost by accident that Jo Davidson, recognized today as America's greatest contemporary sculptor, turned to clay and bronze after setting out to be a painter. While visiting his brother-in-law in New Haven, Davidson noticed a photograph of the newly-appointed president of Yale University. He made a burnt wood portrait from the picture and sold it for $25, his first earned fee as an artist. But what was more important, his drawings were shown to the head of the Yale Art School. He was so impressed that he invited the young man to come and work with him. Although Davidson had no money, he was accepted without any fees.

One day, while wandering through the art school, Davidson stumbled across a room full of plaster casts and modeling stands. He found the clay bin, scooped out a fistful of damp clay, and began to shape it. It was the start of a career which was to see Jo Davidson create busts of practically every great man and woman in the world—Roosevelt and Wilson, Pershing, Joffre, Foch, Bernard Shaw, H. G. Wells, John D. Rockefeller, Walt Whitman, Sir James Barrie, and hundreds more. At the height of his career, he came to be known as a thinker in bronze and a poet in clay.

In the beginning, Jo Davidson had had hard going. Born on New York's East Side in 1883, he had been dreadfully poor. His father, descendant of a long line of scholars and rabbis, spent most of his time in prayer. It was with difficulty that his mother could persuade young Jo to finish grammar school. Instead of studying, Jo preferred to draw. At 14, he was working at various jobs, stealing what little time he could to attend art classes at the Educational Alliance. Finally he won a scholarship at the Art Students League. There followed the Yale episode, and later his first commission to make a portrait bust. In 1907, Davidson left for Paris and travel abroad. In 1910, he returned to the United States to give his first American exhibit. From that time, the commissions came thick and fast. Many of his pieces have become permanent additions to the great museums of the world as well as cherished items in the finest private collections.

[35]

Benjamin
DISRAELI

Prime Minister Of England

Few Jews in modern times have played so vital a part in world affairs as Benjamin Disraeli. First Jew to become Prime Minister of England, Disraeli was the son of a wealthy Spanish Jew. At school as a boy, he suffered much from the taunts and jeers of his fellow-pupils. But he protected himself with his sturdy fists and his witty tongue. At 15, his formal education ended, but he continued to read and study with intense concentration, determined to learn as much as he could so that he could realize his dream of a great career.

He entered a solicitor's office to study law when he was 17, but the life bored him. He began to write, and at 21, published the first of a number of distinguished novels. Then, after three defeats, he successfully stood for Parliament and was elected for the first time in 1837. He was hooted down when he made his maiden speech in the House of Commons but was not discouraged. His brilliant mind and political sagacity advanced his cause until at last he became head of the Conservative Party, a post

he held for 25 years. Bills he forwarded in Parliament provided for shortening the hours of labor, for protection of children in factories, and improvement of housing for the poor.

When he was 63, Queen Victoria made him Prime Minister of England. In the ensuing 3 years, Disraeli did more for his country than had been done in almost half a century before him.

He provided Canada with a charter of liberty and progress. He purchased the Suez Canal, brought India under the Crown and made Victoria Empress of India.

In 1876, Disraeli was made a peer of England with the title of Lord Beaconsfield. He was awarded the coveted Order of the Garter, and became leader of the House of Lords.

When he died in 1881, all England mourned the man who had once been jeered and insulted as a Jew. He had created a great British Empire through his skill and diplomacy. Though he was offered burial with England's great in Westminster Abbey, Disraeli, by his own wish, was laid to rest beside the body of his faithful and loving wife.

Samuel DREBEN

A Soldier Of Fortune

Sam Dreben was born in the Ukrainian town of Poltava in 1878. His father wanted him to study to be a rabbi, but a life of scholarship and teaching did not appeal to him. He ran away from home and eventually came to America.

He was a short squat lad of 18 when he joined the United States army. He quickly won a reputation as a fighting man. When the Spanish-American War broke out in 1898, Sam was shipped out to the Philippines. In his first battle in Cavite province, Sam Dreben charged alone into an army of 2,000 fanatical, bloodthirsty Moros who were threatening to overcome his outfit. Dreben's daring action turned the tide of a losing battle as the rebellious natives broke ranks in disorder and fled for their lives.

After that campaign, Dreben fought all over the world. He became one of the most colorful soldiers of fortune, serving in the American uniform in China during the Boxer Rebellion, in Nicaragua, Honduras, Venezuela and Mexico. Wherever he went, he seemed to lead a charmed life. Captured during the campaign against Pancho Villa in Mexico, Sam was placed before a firing squad. When the order of execution was given, the soldiers turned their weapons instead on their own commanding officer. In Nicaragua, where Sam was wounded seriously, he jested as he lay on what was supposed to be his deathbed. "I can't die now," he said. "I'm a good Jew and there's no Jewish cemetery here!"

Fully recovered when World War I came along, Sam was, as usual, in the forefront of the action. He won the prized Distinguished Service Cross for rushing an enemy post and killing 23 of the 40 Germans in it. He drew from General Pershing, commander-in-chief of all the American troops, the remark, "He is my bravest and finest soldier."

Sam Dreben won several more medals for gallantry in action during World War I to go with the many he had already been awarded over the years for his stirring deeds. When he died in 1925, at the early age of 52, still jesting at death, he had achieved the unusual distinction of having served his country as a fighting soldier in more wars than any other Jew in history.

Paul
EHRLICH

He Fired A Magic Bullet

As a young doctor in Germany, Paul Ehrlich seemed destined to live and work in obscurity. He had entered the profession of medicine with little enthusiasm, and had been a rather mediocre student in a field he had embraced on his mother's insistence. But there was something that Ehrlich was looking for to help cure disease, and he devoted the major part of his life to finding it. His idea was that it was possible to find chemical compounds which could be used to destroy germs in the body. He invented the word chemotherapy to fit his idea, and began to look for such compounds as would attack disease without harming healthy body tissues. He thus set himself a stupendous task— but he conquered it. To those who laughed at his insistence that chemical means could be found to counteract disease in the body he had one simple answer. "We must learn to shoot microbes with magic bullets," were his words. And he continued to experiment.

The disease that Ehrlich eventually determined to meet head on was the scourge of syphilis, one of the worst maimers and killers of the time. He prepared compound after compound without success until he had made 605 of them. Then, with his 606th experiment, Ehrlich at last succeeded in putting together a chemical compound that he called salvarsan that was effective against the ancient disease. And to it, the doctors who had scoffed at Ehrlich's work for so many fruitless years gave the nickname of "the magic bullet."

With his discovery, Paul Ehrlich crowned more than ten years of feverish work in the laboratory. In person, he was an owlish little man, gay and impulsive, who had barely survived tuberculosis which struck him in his 30's. At 45, he had still been a failure. But with the discovery of his cure for syphilis, Ehrlich achieved world-wide fame and the Nobel Prize. The new acclaim made little difference to him or his way of life, for he continued to work until he was old and ill, dying at last in his laboratory. Without his theory of the use of chemical compounds as bullets against disease, modern medicine would not be in its golden age today.

$$m = \frac{m_0}{\sqrt{1 - \frac{v^2}{c^2}}}$$

Albert EINSTEIN

The Thinker Who Changed The World

One of the greatest thinkers of all time was born in a small German city in March, 1879. His early years were hardly indicative of what Albert Einstein was to become and what his discoveries were to mean to civilization. As a child, he seemed mentally backward and could hardly learn to speak. But at six, he developed a passion for music and could play the violin quite well, as he continued to do all his life.

Little Albert hated school, found little sympathy at home, and was terribly lonely. His schoolwork was poor except in mathematics for which he seemed to have a special aptitude. By the time he was 13, he was being recognized as a mathematical genius, but was otherwise little fitted for ordinary living.

He at first failed the entrance examinations to the university at Zurich, Switzerland, but was finally admitted and graduated. Because he had to make a living, he went to work in the government patent office at Berne. In his free time, he studied physics. And when he was 26, in 1905, he developed and published his first work on relativity.

He taught for a while at the University of Zurich and his reputation began to spread. In 1915, he issued his General Theory of Relativity and it created a revolution in thought unprecedented in the history of science.

In 1921, Albert Einstein was awarded the coveted Nobel Prize. And when Hitler took over Germany, Einstein, a refugee without home or possessions, fled to America where he became a member of the Institute for Advanced Study at Princeton and continued to seek out the secrets of the universe.

It was his famous letter to President Roosevelt that started the making of the atom bomb, a discovery that stemmed directly from his own theory of the nature of matter and energy.

Having spent his entire lifetime explaining the workings of the universe, the shy and retiring genius died in 1955, at 76. Even then his thoughts were only for science. For in his will, Einstein left his brain to science, the brain that had revolutionized human thought and given birth to the atomic age.

ELIJAH
(The Gaon of Vilna)

The Gaon of Vilna

Born as Elijah ben Solomon in 1720 in the city of Vilna, Lithuania, the Gaon of Vilna, as he came to be called, was marked almost from birth as the most brilliant scholar of his age among the Jewish people. At the age of 7 he was already so keen of mind that he was capable of delivering a sparkling homily before an assembly of great scholars. When several Poles who had heard so much about the child prodigy of learning tried to kidnap him for ransom, the boy was saved and sent for safety to another city, Brest-Litovsk, where he stayed and studied with the best teachers till he was 25.

When he returned to Vilna, the community invited him to become their rabbi. But he did not want a public position. He sought only an opportunity for quiet study. Nevertheless, he was acknowledged as the spiritual head not only of Vilna but of all European Jewry. His opinions became as laws for the people. And he was given the honorary title of Gaon, a title that had been borne by the heads of the great Babylonian academies a thousand years before.

By the time he was 40, the Gaon had written more than 70 major works. Among them were commentaries on the Bible, treatises on Biblical geography, textbooks on astronomy and mathematics, and a grammar of the Hebrew language.

He became famous for his ability to decide the weightiest problems in an instant, problems that had troubled other leading scholars for months. His brilliant mind and saintly character affected Jewish thought not only in his own time but to this very day.

The Gaon surrounded himself with many devoted students. Basic to his teaching was the precept that one must never accept blindly the explanations of others, not even of the greatest of scholars. Always go to the original source, he taught them, study it until you understand it thoroughly. As for the Talmud, the Gaon instructed his pupils that it must be interpreted on the basis of reason and common sense and not authority.

While his own life was a constant attempt to perfect his own character, he also strove to lift the spirits and better the minds of his people. When he passed away in 1797, the Gaon of Vilna, revered by all, had won enduring fame as the greatest scholar in Hebrew history.

Queen
ESTHER

She Was Once A Queen

When the mighty Ahaseurus was King of all the land between India and Ethiopia, there lived in his capital city of Susa a Jew named Mordecai who was the foster father of the lovely Esther. When a day came that Ahaseurus sought as wife and queen the most beautiful maiden in all his kingdom, hundreds of girls were sent to his court for him to choose from. Among them was Esther, whose name in Persian is Hadassah. It was the world's first beauty contest.

Esther's beauty and dignity of bearing greatly impressed the King Ahaseurus, and he made her his queen amid much pomp and ceremony. But she did not tell him that she and her foster father, Mordecai, were Jews.

One day, Mordecai learned of a plot to assassinate the King. He sent word of the conspiracy to Queen Esther. She, in turn, passed it on to the King. The plot was smashed and the evil plotters punished.

Then the King made Haman his Prime Minister, and Haman came to hate the Jew, Mordecai, because he would not bow before him. And he prevailed on Ahaseurus to issue a decree to kill all the Jews in the kingdom.

When Mordecai heard of this terrible plan, he told Esther that the time had come for her to help her people. And Esther, though she faced the death penalty for approaching the King without permission, went in to Ahaseurus and told him how Haman was plotting against the Jews and that they were her people. Meanwhile, the King had learned that Mordecai, who had saved his life, had received no recompense for his service to the King.

So the mighty Ahaseurus ordered that Mordecai and all the Jews be spared, but that Haman be hanged on the very gallows that had been intended for the foster father of his Queen. And the Jews rejoiced in their deliverance and sang many praises of Queen Esther. A festival to commemorate the occasion was ordained and it has come down to us as the Feast of Purim. Each year at the same time all Jews celebrate joyfully the memory of her courage and devotion and the destruction of Haman, man of evil design.

Only two books in Holy Scripture honor Jewish women by being named for them. One of these is Ruth. The other is the brave and beautiful Esther.

Edna
FERBER

Lady Of Letters

When Edna Ferber was a little girl in Appleton, Wisconsin, the thought furthest from her mind was that she might some day become a writer. In her family, the children were attracted to the theatre rather than any other form of expression. When she won a declamation prize at school, Edna Ferber set her mind on studying speech and elocution. Unfortunately, her father, a Hungarian Jew who had not been particularly successful in business, went blind. To help the family, an unhappy, frustrated and dissatisfied Edna Ferber took a job as a local reporter on the town paper at $3 a week.

A year or so later, a new city editor fired her, and she went on to Milwaukee where she got a somewhat better job on the *Journal*. For the following four years, she did a man's work on the paper as a reporter. When her father died, she went on to Chicago and landed on the *Tribune* there. In her spare time, she tried her hand at creative writing. She completed a novel but did not like it and cast it aside. Her mother rescued the manuscript from the dustbin and sent it to a publisher. It was snapped up, and in

1911 was published and sold over 10,000 copies. A great career was under way.

From that time, many stories, novels and plays poured from the fertile mind of Edna Ferber. Her novels have soared to the best-seller class again and again. Among them were such well-known titles as "Saratoga Trunk," "So Big," "Cimarron," "Show Boat." Her short stories won her the love and respect of millions of magazine readers. As a playwright, she won over Broadway with such smash hits as "The Royal Family," "Dinner At Eight," "Stage Door," and again "Show Boat," which proved to be one of the greatest stage and film stories ever seen or heard. Later, there was her autobiography, "A Peculiar Treasure," the story not only of her American Jewish family and its place in a free land, but also a powerful indictment of the anti-Semitism which had almost destroyed Europe and threatened an unwary America.

Edna Ferber has received many honors as one of America's leading literary figures, among them membership in the National Institute of Arts and Letters and an honorary degree from Columbia University.

Dr.
Abraham
FLEXNER

Medical Educator

Though Simon Flexner made tremendous contributions to medical research, his younger brother, Abraham, won greater fame as the man who revolutionized medical education methods. Many a hospital patient today owes his very life to Abraham Flexner and his passion for the improvement of medical schools.

Born into a family of pious Jews in Louisville, Kentucky, Abraham found himself, at 19, teaching in high school. Four years later, in 1890, he decided to put his own ideas into practice. He started his own school, following his own methods of no examinations, no records or reports, and no fixed speed of study.

College authorities soon began to notice that Flexner's pupils were reaching their campuses at an earlier age and better prepared. But with success assured, Flexner suddenly gave up the school to continue his own studies at Harvard and Berlin. In 1908, on his return to America, the Carnegie Foundation asked him to make a survey of American medical schools.

What Flexner found out appalled him. His report, published in 1910, was a veritable bombshell dropped on the medical world. It was only the first in a series of such studies by him on professional education, all of which had a profound influence. In 1915, he framed a plan for a model school which was subsequently established as the famous Lincoln Experimental School at Teachers College.

But it was with the financing of modern medical education that Abraham Flexner's name is irrevocably linked. In answer to his personal appeal, John D. Rockefeller, Sr., gave fifty million dollars to reorganize American medical education. Then he induced such great men of wealth as Andrew Carnegie, Julius Rosenwald, George Eastman, J. P. Morgan and others to give more than half a billion dollars for medical schools both in America and Europe.

Finally, he persuaded Louis Bamberger, the celebrated Jewish department store owner, to give eight million dollars for the establishment of the Institute for Advanced Study at Princeton University. Flexner himself became the first director of that great institution for the most brilliant minds in the world. He remained its director for nine years, until he retired so that he could travel and lecture.

Founder of the Institute for Advanced Study was the crowning honor for the man who had, singlehanded, been responsible for modern medical education and had found the money to make it possible.

Always, he will be remembered as the Father of Modern Medical Education.

Pierre MENDÈS-FRANCE

A Leader For France

In the summer of 1940, after the downfall of France, a lieutenant of the French Air Force, by the name of Pierre Mendes-France, was branded a deserter from the French Army by the officials of the traitorous Vichy Government. He was arrested and sentenced to six years in prison at hard labor. But he escaped to join Charles de Gaulle's Free French Forces so as to continue to fight against Germany until its final defeat, and until unhappy France was liberated.

In the summer of 1954, almost to the very same day when he had suffered the humiliation of being branded a French traitor and sent to prison for his crime, Pierre Mendes-France was called upon to become the leader of his country. At the age of 47, he became Premier of France, one of the youngest in history.

Quickly, he achieved international fame as a statesman for universal respect. For during the next 7 months and 17 days, he compiled such a sensational record as the Premier of France that the leaders of the world spoke in admiration of him as a "superman" statesman. In rapid succession, he ended the disastrous war in Indochina which was bleeding France, he scrapped the European Defense Community treaty, drafted and signed the new Paris treaties, solved the burning Tunis colonial problem, and he proposed sweeping economic reforms for all

France. Fearful of his rapid growth as the strong man of France, powerful political opponents combined against him, and finally, his government fell. But for most Frenchmen, Pierre Mendes-France has remained their leader of the future who will guide their tragic country to the dawn of a new glory.

Born in Paris in 1907, Pierre Mendes-France is descended from a long line of Sephardic Jewish dealers in cloth. His maternal grandmother, a devout orthodox Jew, was responsible for his early religious training. At 18, he received his doctor's degree in law, finishing at the head of a class of 800. It was during his student years that he received his broken and misshapen nose in a street brawl with Royalist followers.

He passed the bar examination at 21, becoming the youngest lawyer in all France. He set up practice in Louviers with a view to entering politics as soon as he could become eligible for office. In 1932, Pierre Mendes-France became France's youngest member of the Chamber of Deputies. He remained one for 22 years. In 1934, he was elected Mayor of Louviers. He continued in that office for 20 years until he became the Premier of France.

A brilliant lawyer, a celebrated economist, a scholar and an intellectual, Pierre Mendes-France has filled many important posts in the national government. He has become known as the merciless gadfly of French politics.

Felix FRANKFURTER

The Socrates of the Law

When, in 1939, President Franklin D. Roosevelt nominated him as Associate Justice of the United States Supreme Court, Felix Frankfurter was bitterly attacked by reactionaries as an alien, a radical, and a Jew. However, the little giant of the legal profession—he is only 65 inches tall—deeply impressed the Senate with his sharp, incisive mind and his powerful grasp of the law. In 12 days, his appointment was confirmed without a dissenting vote. Felix Frankfurter joined the Supreme Court as the third Jew in history to hold a seat on that exalted tribunal. And, in 1956, he was the only living Jew on the Supreme Court where his decisions for 17 years have established him, in the opinion of many, as its dominant member.

Felix Frankfurter was born in Vienna in 1882, the descendant of men who had been rabbis for three centuries. His father left the theological seminary to come to the United States where he became a fur merchant. Felix attended public school on the East Side and did odd jobs after school. His earnings were set aside by his mother for his college education.

He graduated from the College of the City of New York at 19 and went on to Harvard to study law, earning his degree in 1906. Eight years later, after showing brilliance in the law both privately and as a law officer for the War Department, he became a professor at the Harvard Law School. So remarkable a teacher was he that even his lodgings came to be called "the house of truth," because of the earnest discussions held there.

Several United States Presidents found occasion to seek his advice, and he became known far and wide as "the Socrates of the Law." As a teacher at Harvard, he turned out scores of brilliant lawyers who went on to hold the highest positions in the land. And while he was only a humble and little-known college professor, his advice was sought and given without fee on vital labor legislation, important social welfare, and celebrated civil liberty cases.

Felix Frankfurter who only wanted to be a college law professor was finally persuaded by the President of the United States to give up his beloved classroom for the higher service to his country. Now for the past 17 years, he has been Mr. Justice Frankfurter, mightiest little giant of the law, and the only Jew wearing the honored robes of a member of the United States Supreme Court.

[45]

Sidney
FRANKLIN

The Matador From Brooklyn

Among the great Jewish figures in the world of sports, Sidney Franklin holds not only a high but also a unique place. For he is the only bullfighter the Jewish people have ever boasted among their number. And far from being an obscure matador of the bull ring, Franklin was truly one of the great artists in a field where skill and daring are so highly prized.

Franklin did not set out in life to be a bullfighter. Born and bred in Brooklyn, New York, he ran off to Mexico as a boy after a quarrel at home. There he set up an art shop where he made and sold posters.

One day, when a friend taunted him with the remark that he would not dare to fight bulls, Franklin wrote to a famous matador and asked many questions about the sport. What he learned about the bull ring fascinated him. To be able to travel all over the world, to earn large fees for fighting bulls, to be an idol of the great crowds who adored bullfighters, appealed to him enormously.

So Sidney Franklin set out to learn bullfighting. He starved and struggled, but persisted until he had become one of the most skillful and graceful matadors the sport had ever seen. He soon became an idol of the followers of the sport in Mexico and Spain where his cold, serene, intelligent valor in the ring delighted the spectators. Often, he was carried from the ring on the shoulders of the fans, an honor accorded only to the greatest matadors. Once, when badly gored by a bull, Franklin amazed them by returning to the ring while his wound was still unhealed.

Sidney Franklin engaged in the perilous sport he loved for 20 years. Many times was he injured and he underwent five operations to recover from serious wounds. So great was his fame that he received a great official reception when he at last returned to America and home. The bullfighter from Brooklyn had made an imperishable place for himself among the honored artists of the bull ring, and no history of the sport can ever be complete unless it gives him the space to which he is entitled.

Sigmund FREUD

Father Of Psychoanalysis

Sigmund Freud was born in Freiberg, Germany, on May 6, 1856. As a boy, he was a brilliant student. He studied the biology of rare fishes for some years, but then, due to financial difficulties, gave up his laboratory for clinical medicine when he was 26. He specialized in clinical neurology and began to work in a children's clinic studying the brain and nerve diseases of childhood.

When he turned to curing patients by the use of hypnosis, Freud caused an uproar among his colleagues in Vienna. Deserted by his friends and fellow-doctors, Freud suddenly conceived of a brilliant idea. Why not try to cure the nervous patient without hypnosis by having him analyze the depths of his own unconscious mind with the doctor's help?

Thus was psychoanalysis born in the great mind of Sigmund Freud. From that point, he developed his theories of the unconscious and a method to bring man's repressed thoughts to the surface of his conscious mind.

For ten years, Freud stood alone with his ideas, neglected and scorned by the world of medicine. At last, recognition came in 1906, and with it many disciples and streams of patients. Today, Freud's method, in one form or another, is accepted as an indispensable tool for the treatment of mental and nervous disorders. When he died in 1939, Freud was an almost legendary giant of medicine, and his passing was commemorated all over the world. And in Vienna, where he once had been scorned and ostracized for his mad ideas, his statue now stands in the court of the University. At its base are inscribed the following words:

SIGMUND FREUD
Who divined the famed riddle and was a man most mighty.

Benny
FRIEDMAN

The Perfect Quarterback

Among Jews who have won fame in the world of sports, no one was ever accorded more national respect and admiration for his ability than Benny Friedman, greatest of Jewish football players. Though many years have passed since he last appeared on the football field, Friedman is remembered vividly as the perfect quarterback. Even his coach, the great Fielding Yost of Michigan, exclaimed that Benny Friedman never made a mistake on the field. No higher tribute could ever be paid a football player.

Friedman's quarterbacking began when he was a star with his high school team in Cleveland, and continued with ever-increasing brilliance in 1925 and 1926 with the University of Michigan. So amazing a player was he that on the two occasions when he faced the immortal

All-America, Red Grange of Illinois, reputed to be the greatest back of them all, little Benny Friedman clearly outplayed that great star.

It was not only as a field general guiding his team that Friedman excelled. He could kick and run with the best of them. His ability was rewarded when he was chosen All-America quarterback by all the experts in the land at a time when all-star choices really meant something. As a 60-minute player in an age of giants, Friedman dearly won his spurs on the gridiron.

After his brilliant college career ended, Benny Friedman entered the professional ranks and for 8 years scintillated as a passer, kicker, runner and brilliant field general. When through with playing, he entered the coaching ranks. In 1956, he was still at it, as the coach of the ever-improving football team of Jewish-supported Brandeis University in Massachusetts.

George
GERSHWIN

An American and His Music

George Gershwin was born in Brooklyn, New York, on September 26, 1898. He died in Hollywood, California, on July 11, 1937. Between those two dates and places, he became the most famous composer America ever produced.

As a boy, George was typical of big city youth. He was athletic, played games, was even roller-skating champion of his neighborhood. He was rough, tough and mean to kids who played the piano.

Then the Gershwins bought a second-hand piano so Ira, George's older brother, could take lessons. In a few weeks, George had crowded him away from the instrument. Only 13, he begged his mother to get him a piano teacher.

With the world of music suddenly opened to him, George began to haunt music halls. At 14, he wrote his first song. Nobody bought it. He listened to the tunes of Irving Berlin, Jerome Kern, the classics. Everything he heard he soaked up like a sponge.

At 16, he left school and went to work as a song-plugger for a music publishing firm. When they refused to listen to the tunes he wrote himself, he quit. And when he was 18, he finally sold his first song—for $5.

But then he wrote a number called

"Swanee," and he became famous and wealthy almost overnight when Al Jolson sang it and brought the house down. Now George began to turn out song hit after song hit. Money poured in. He wrote "Rhapsody in Blue" which was played in Carnegie Hall and established him as a serious American artist. He now lived in two worlds, Tin Pan Alley and the concert hall. For every smash musical he wrote for Broadway, there was a serious piece for Carnegie Hall.

When he was 37, George Gershwin wrote the opera "Porgy and Bess." It created a sensation. Its great music and stirring drama moved audiences to tears and cheers. Twenty years later, it was still bringing the wildest acclaim all over the world. In 1956, it pierced the Iron Curtain and was presented for the first time in Russia, and that country went wild over Gershwin's great American masterpiece.

But he was not to know about that. For brief was his journey to greatness. In 1937, in his 39th year, the composer of America's greatest native opera, and the only universally-accepted American opera, suddenly died. Never, in the years since, have his songs or compositions been silent or unsung. The passage of time has only added fame and glory to the memory of America's greatest and most universally-popular composer, George Gershwin.

Adam GIMBEL

Father Of The Department Store

One somehow tends to forget that behind the name of a great merchandising empire like Gimbel's there was once a man. That man was Adam Gimbel, the pioneer merchant who founded the department store as we know it today.

When Adam Gimbel was only 18, he left Bavaria and poverty to come to America. Landing in New Orleans, penniless and alone, he found arduous and ill-paid work on the docks. He learned a little English and began to look around him for a better way of life. He heard that people who lived away from the cities were clamoring for the kinds of goods they could not obtain in their bleak wilderness. With the money he saved by scraping and pinching, Gimbel bought up a variety of goods, including needles, pins, thimbles, ribbons, knives, tobacco, broadcloth, combs and clocks. Then young Adam, the peddler, flung the pack over his shoulder and set out, rifle in hand, for the Mississippi Valley. Thus, modestly, began one of America's great empires of trade.

After a few years of incredible hardship, eased only by the many friends he made among the trappers, Indians and river men, Gimbel decided to settle down in one place. At 25, he opened a small shop in Vincennes, Indiana, and became a storekeeper—but a most unusual storekeeper. First, he drew up and distributed a handbill to advertise the opening of his new establishment. Such a thing had never been done before. Then he set up policies for the store's operation that were really different. He insisted that all customers, rich and poor, white and Indian, receive the same prompt and courteous service. More startling still, he offered to refund the purchase price to any customer dissatisfied with what he bought. These novel ideas, as well as fixed prices and honest description of goods, brought customers flocking to the store. Because most of them could not come in as often as they would have liked, Gimbel made their buying easy by stocking up with a great many varieties of wares under the single roof, thus making his place the first modern department store.

The store prospered, and Adam Gimbel's seven sons spread the gospel of the department store across the land. But as big as Gimbel's may be today, it all goes back to the man who was first a peddler of notions and then pioneered America's first department store.

Alma GLUCK

Songbird Of The Opera

Only a handful of Jewish women have been gifted with voices rich enough to bring them international fame in grand opera. Among them were such great stars as Sophie Breslau, Rosa Raisa, Jennie Tourel, Regina Resnik, Dorothy Sarnoff and Roberta Peters. The greatest and most famous of them all, however, was Alma Gluck.

Born in Bucharest in 1884, the then Reba Fierson came as a small child to New York. Her childhood was uneventful with no hint of a musical career in the future. After finishing school, she went to work as a stenographer. Later, she married Bernard Gluck.

One summer, while vacationing at a mountain resort, the social director asked her to participate in an amateur stage show. She volunteered to sing a song. Facing her first audience, the untrained girl made a deep impression. A guest told her to go to a teacher for voice training. Wishing only to improve her voice for her own pleasure, Alma Gluck agreed.

The music teacher who heard her for the first time was enthralled by the pure, rich, natural voice of Alma Gluck. What started out as lessons for fun turned into serious business as the teacher insisted that she train to become an opera singer.

After three years of hard work, the teacher arranged for her to sing for a friend of his. When it was over, she was amazed to learn that the friend was Arturo Toscanini, world-famed opera conductor. Toscanini was so impressed by the beauty of her voice that he promptly recommended that she be engaged by the Metropolitan Opera.

Alma Gluck made her debut on November 6, 1909, and scored a phenomenal and instant success. Her enchanting voice, her personality and manner, captivated the audience. She sped from success to success, on the concert stage as well as in opera. And she found lasting happiness in her marriage to the great violinist, Efrem Zimbalist.

When her singing days were over, the incomparable Alma Gluck devoted herself to helping young and needy artists on their way to fame and fortune in music. In 1938, death wrote finis to the glorious career of Alma Gluck, most fabulously successful of Jewish opera singers.

Dr. JOSEPH GOLDBERGER

He Conquered A Disease Of The Poor

It was, in a sense, almost an accident that set Joseph Goldberger on the path that was to lead him to the conquest of pellagra, the mysterious ailment that was taking thousands of lives in the Southern states. Having been brought to this country from Austria at the age of 6, Joseph Goldberger started to study engineering at the College of the City of New York. A friend invited him to hear a lecture by a physiology professor at Bellevue Medical School. Goldberger was fascinated. He gave up engineering and entered Bellevue as a medical student.

When he graduated, he began to practice in a small town, but felt unsatisfied with what he was doing. His heart was set on doing medical research, and when he learned that the U.S. Marine Hospital Service had vacancies to fill, he took the examination and passed. He was to spend the next 30 years in the field of public health and medical research.

For a few years, Goldberger did notable research on a number of public health problems, but finally he was assigned to do pellagra studies in the South. Until his time, pellagra had been considered a disease caused by germs and contagious in nature. But Goldberger thought otherwise. He was certain that pellagra was due to poor and improper food, and had nothing to do with germs or any other source of disease. In short, he felt that pellagra was an affliction of the poor, a disease of starvation. And to prove his point to the many skeptics who scorned his idea, Goldberger permitted himself and his wife to be injected with the blood of a pellagra victim. If the disease was germ-caused, he would be stricken with it. But Goldberger did not fall ill of pellagra. Now he could maintain with complete assurance that the sickness was caused by the lack of a certain food factor which he called Pellagra-Preventative, or P.P., and that it could be found in foods that the sufferers from pellagra lacked most: lean beef, milk, eggs, and green leafy vegetables.

To honor Joseph Goldberger, who died penniless at 54, the factor he discovered that would prevent pellagra was renamed Vitamin G.

Edwin Franko GOLDMAN

Strike Up The Band

It is generally held that the most famous band leader of all was the ever-loved John Philip Sousa. However, one who achieved as much fame and was universally recognized the superior musician was Edwin Franko Goldman, born in Louisville, Kentucky, 1878. Even the widow of John Philip Sousa acknowledged that Goldman had a right to take her husband's place as the world's greatest band leader when she presented him with her late husband's favorite baton.

Goldman was born into a musical family. His mother, a child violin and piano prodigy, had won fame as a concert artist in America and Europe. His father, a lawyer, was also a talented pianist. But at 8, young Edwin then a schoolboy in New York, began playing an instrument strange to both his parents. Anxious to play in his public school band, to join it, he had to buy a cornet. Fascinated by the shiny horn, he drove his parents and the neighbors to distraction by his constant tootling.

After two years of such torturous practice, he suddenly found himself popular and in demand everywhere as a solo cornetist. At 15, he won a scholarship to the National Conservatory. At 17, he was the first cornetist for the famed Metropolitan Opera Orchestra. They called him "the baby of the Met."

For 10 years, Goldman played in the Metropolitan Orchestra pit. In 1912, he left the opera to teach. Pupils flocked to him from all over the world to study the cornet and trumpet. At the same time, he began to conduct free band concerts.

Dissatisfied with the poor musical quality of most bands, he organized his own group of personally trained musicians. It became known as the Goldman Band—the finest musical organization in band history. Proudly, the world's leading composers wrote music especially for the Goldman Band, for he had created a symphony orchestra in brass.

Franko Goldman became universally famous as the maker of music for the masses. For 38 years, in parks and auditoriums all over the world, he conducted free concerts, and the Goldman Band was heard by more people than any other band in musical history.

He was the first musician ever to receive official honors from the City of New York, as well as Boston, San Francisco, Toronto, and many other large cities thruout America and Canada. Many European countries also honored him, while Universities conferred honorary degrees upon him in recognition of him as a bandleader and a musician.

He wrote over 100 marches and numerous other compositions. His march, "On the Mall," is considered equal in popularity to Sousa's "Stars and Stripes Forever."

He was preparing to conduct his 2,147th consecutive concert, when he died at 78.

Samuel GOLDWYN

He Found Hollywood

Born in poverty in Warsaw, Poland, in 1879, Samuel Goldfish found himself an orphan at 11. He ran away from his parentless home and came to London where he worked in a blacksmith shop for several years. Then at 14, he left England, and alone, he made his way to America.

In his early years in New York, he was a glove salesman. So capable did he prove to be that while still in his early twenties, he was earning $15,000 a year. He was the best glove salesman in that trade.

However, he became fascinated with the nickelodeons which were so popular at the time, and he pestered his brother-in-law, Jesse Lasky, a pioneer in the movie business, to make motion pictures with him. He had a then-crazy idea that full length stories and stage plays could be made into motion pictures.

In 1913, he gave up being a successful glove salesman, changed his name to Samuel Goldwyn, and went into the business of making motion pictures. He rented a stable, and produced the first feature-length motion picture ever made. It was called, "The Squaw Man."

In those early pioneering days, all motion pictures were made in the East, mostly indoors. Samuel Goldwyn bursting with fantastic plans for picture-making wanted to find a more suitable place with good climate for the making of outdoor movies the year round. He went West and found such a place. It turned out to be Hollywood, now the world-center of movie making. More than any one else, Samuel Goldwyn was responsible for founding Hollywood.

He became the most fabulous and the most fantastically successful independent motion picture producer in history. For over 35 years, he made the finest pictures in the world, and he produced many screen classics, like, "The Best Years of Our Lives" which won more Academy Award Oscars than any other single film ever did.

No one spent more to get the best actors, writers and directors than Goldwyn. He was the first to pay as much as one million dollars for a story to film. Although, he introduced to the world many of the most famous screen stars in motion picture history, he has remained the only producer whose name on a theatre marquee means as much as the star's.

He has earned a fortune of millions, and he has gained an eminent place in the film world. His pictures have won the highest awards for excellence, and yet, the best of his pictures have been no more exciting or gripping or fascinating than Samuel Goldwyn's own career as a motion picture pioneer.

Samuel GOMPERS

His Life For Labor's Cause

As a small boy in the England where he was born, Sam Gompers was forced by poverty to leave school at the age of ten. He was apprenticed to a shoemaker who paid the hungry child six cents a week. Soon unemployment drove the boy's father to emigrate to New York. There, in a filthy sweatshop on the teeming East Side, Sam learned the craft of cigar making and grew to manhood. At the age of 24, he was earning only $12 a week.

Through the years of suffering, Sam learned how important it was for workingmen to act together and how much power they had when they did so. And no strike he ever organized ever gave him more satisfaction than his first one—to help an old blind cigar maker regain his choice seat near the window in the dingy and airless cigar factory where they worked. The strike was won.

From that beginning, Sam went on to develop his ideas about the relationship between workers and employers until he had clearly in his mind the objective to which he was to devote the rest of his life—a big organization of workers who would stand together to improve

their working conditions and thereby attain richer and fuller lives.

In 1886, after ten years of advocating his holy cause, Sam finally founded the American Federation of Labor. He became its first president and held that office for the following forty years.

As the A.F.L. grew stronger and bigger, Sam came to be acknowledged everywhere as the spokesman for the American worker and labor's most famous champion. When he visited England, the land that had given him birth, even the King received him as an honored guest at the palace.

Though often tempted with flattering offers from industry, Sam never considered leaving his beloved A.F.L. and the modest salary it paid him. Comparatively poor all his life, Sam Gompers was rich in the love and gratitude of the millions of American workers who owed him so much for what he achieved for them. Today the American Federation of Labor is the most powerful labor organization in the world. And America's workers live better and happier lives, thanks to the onetime cigar maker who devoted his life to their cause.

Benny
GOODMAN

King Of Swing

Benny Goodman was born in 1909 in a Chicago slum where his father was a poor tailor who could hardly earn a living for his brood of youngsters. One day Benny's father heard that a boys' band was being formed at a neighborhood synagogue. Membership in the band included free musical training, so Benny and his two brothers were enrolled in the new organization. As the smallest of the boys, Benny was forced to accept the instrument that no one else wanted. It was a clarinet.

Mr. Goodman made sure that his little son practiced hard and often. In the winter time, he dragged Benny by sled to rehearsals so he would not have to walk. Then when he was 12, Benny heard his first jazz music on a cheap phonograph his father had bought him. He was enchanted. He began to play jazz, to study the obscure and little-known masters of the form. He organized a boys' band and took them into the woods where they played hour after hour jazz variations on the popular tunes of the day.

He was only 15 when he got his first im-portant job as clarinetist in a band. He stayed with it for some years but finally Benny organized his own outfit and went out to play his new swing music before a public that took to him at once. He was crowned King of Swing and immense audiences flocked to hear him. Swing became a national passion. No public music idol had ever before received such wild receptions from young people.

Benny Goodman achieved world-wide fame as King of Swing, but there was also a serious side to his music that came to be appreciated almost as much. He played solo with some of the greatest symphonic orchestras in the world, and the critics called him one of the greatest artists of the clarinet that had ever lived.

But it is mainly for his swing music that Benny Goodman remains famous. He started a veritable landslide of jazz orchestras that swept across the country in his wake, and it is mainly his doing that jazz has come to be accepted as America's authentic contribution to the music of the world.

Rebecca GRATZ

The Beauty Who Glorified All Womanhood

Born in Philadelphia to wealth and high position, Rebecca Gratz was one of the most beautiful and gracious women of her time. To her beauty and grace she added such nobility of spirit and goodness of heart that she was the idol of all who knew her.

With all the world at her feet, Rebecca Gratz unfortunately fell in love with a man not of her faith. As a devout Jew, she could not marry the man of her choice. And though many came later to seek her hand, she remained unmarried all of her long life.

Rather than pine away for a love that she could not bring herself to accept, Rebecca Gratz threw herself into a maze of activities. What she could not do for herself, she could and did do for her fellow-Jew who was less fortunate than herself. She founded the very first Jewish orphan's home in America. She started the Female Hebrew Benevolent Society in 1818. This was a momentous event, for this organization was the first Jewish philanthropic agency apart from a synagogue ever established and was the inspiration for all the Jewish welfare agencies to appear later. Again, she established a Jewish Sunday School for religious education, the first of its kind in America.

Besides all her important religious and philanthropic work, Rebecca Gratz found time to meet and know the great artists and writers of her day. They came from near and far to see and talk to the most beautiful and gracious woman in Philadelphia. Among her most ardent admirers was the famous author, Washington Irving. When Irving went abroad, he met Sir Walter Scott and told that great novelist all about the beautiful, pure-hearted and devout Rebecca Gratz who, to Irving, was a Jewish woman who glorified all womanhood. Fascinated by the glowing description of this wonderful person, Scott immortalized her in the celebrated novel, "Ivanhoe," as the lovely and faithful Rebecca.

Rebecca Gratz died at 87, acclaimed and mourned as the foremost of her faith in the United States. One of the noblest women in the world was laid to rest in Mikvah Israel Cemetery in Philadelphia in 1869.

Hank
GREENBERG

The Baseball Slugger

When he was only a high school boy in New York, the Bronx-born Hank Greenberg was already so outstanding a baseball player, that he attracted the attention of several big league baseball scouts. Impressed by what they saw, the scouts representing the New York Yankees and the Detroit Tigers made tempting offers to the tall and powerful schoolboy to join their clubs and play professional baseball. Since the offers came at the same time, Hank's mother invited the two scouts to come to the Greenberg home and partake of a traditional Friday night supper at an orthodox Romanian Jewish table. She was locally celebrated for her gefulte fish.

Although Hank yearned most to play for his home town team, the fabulous New York Yankees, the scout from that club, a gentile, failed to appear that Friday night, and keep the appointment to come and eat mama Greenberg's gefulte fish. However, the scout from the Detroit club did appear, ate till he could hardly stand, and most graciously praised Mother Greenberg's Jewish cooking to the skies. That so pleased young Hank that he agreed to play baseball for the Detroit Tigers. He was then barely 19.

With that team, Hank Greenberg became

one of baseball's greatest first basemen, and the most famous Jewish baseball hero in history. He became one of the greatest home run sluggers of all time. In the 1938 season, he hit 58 home runs, and in the 13 years he starred in the majors, he hit 331 home runs. He was paid more than $65,000 a year to play baseball.

At the peak of his career, World War II intervened, and Hank became one of the first big leaguers to lay aside his baseball uniform to fight for his country. He served in the Army for four years, rising through the ranks from a private to an officer, before he returned to baseball. Though aged to 34 by then, he resumed his home run slugging and led his team to a pennant. Two years later, he retired from active play, and he became a respected owner of a major league baseball club.

In 1956, ten years after he had played his last baseball game, the greatest honor that can come to a professional baseball player came to Hank Greenberg. He was elected to baseball's exclusive Hall of Fame, the first and only Jewish player ever to be so honored. With this achievement, Hank Greenberg took his place among the immortals of America's national pastime where he will remain enshrined forever as an inspiration to youth.

RODGERS and HAMMERSTEIN

A Musical Marriage Made In Heaven

A marriage of talents as successful as that of the immortal team of Gilbert and Sullivan has brought to the American stage a brand new concept of musical theatre. The phrase "Music by Richard Rodgers, Book and Lyrics by Oscar Hammerstein II" has become a guarantee that the very best music has been wedded to the cleverest words in show business.

Richard Rodgers was born in 1902, the son of a successful New York doctor. His mother, an accomplished pianist, gave him his first piano lessons. Soon, he was able to improvise original melodies. At 14, he had written his first song, and at 15, he wrote his first complete musical score, for an amateur revue. At Columbia University, he wrote the score for the Varsity Show when only a freshman, a feat never before equalled. Later, he teamed up with Lorenz Hart, and during the 23 years of their collaboration, they developed a new art form—the musical play. Their musical plays were fabulously successful, and Richard Rodgers became one of the most successful composers for the theatre in our time.

Then Hart died, and a new brilliant collaboration in the theatre was born—Rodgers and Oscar Hammerstein II.

Born in 1895, Hammerstein also was a New Yorker born and bred. He bore a name of great distinction in the theatre. His grandfather had been the famous opera impresario. His father was a vaudeville producer. His uncle was a musical comedy producer. His brother a stage director, and his cousin a movie star. With so much theatre in his background, young Oscar went to Columbia University—to study law. There, he acted, wrote verse and college shows. In 1917, he took a job as a stage manager with his uncle. He began to write and from his pen came book and lyrics for such successful Broadway shows as "Showboat," "Carmen Jones," "Sunny" and more than a thousand published songs.

Upon Hart's untimely death, Rodgers and Hammerstein teamed up. Their first show was "Oklahoma," which scored a record-breaking run of 2,246 Broadway performances, was presented around the world in various languages for eight years, and was seen by some 20 million people. It earned for them one million dollars.

There followed a bewildering series of great musical shows, "South Pacific," "The King and I," "Carousel," "Pal Joey" and many more. Not for nothing has it been said that the musical marriage of Rodgers and Hammerstein was truly one that was made in show business's heaven. For theirs has been a music partnership which has earned for them a fortune of millions and universal fame, but it also has made their names as immortal as those of Gilbert and Sullivan.

Lillian
HELLMAN

Lady Playwright

The story of the American theatre is rich with Jewish names. No branch of the drama fails to include at least a few of them. As writers for the stage, they have been particularly prominent. It is therefore a high honor indeed for Lillian Hellman to be considered the outstanding playwright in American letters today.

Born in 1905 in New Orleans, Louisiana, Lillian Hellman was brought up in New York where she attended the public schools. After three years at New York University, she found a job in 1924 with a publishing house which paid her the munificent salary of $17.50 a week. A year later, she was reviewing books and helping her husband in his publicity work. Meanwhile, she had decided to make writing her life work.

But her work did not sell, and for a number of discouraging years she read play scripts and movie scenarios while struggling with her writing. At last, success smiled on her efforts. While working for the noted producer, Herman Shumlin—she was reading scripts, as usual— she wrote her own first long play, "The Children's Hour." Mr. Shumlin himself produced it and it was a smash hit on Broadway.

Established at last as a playwright, Lillian

Hellman more than fulfilled the promise of her first play in the years that followed. She traveled extensively in Europe and became an ardent fighter against fascism, actually coming under bombardment in 1937 during the Spanish Civil War. She wrote stirringly against the scourge that was to see its apex in the infamous Hitler regime. For as once she wrote, "I am a writer and I am also a Jew. I want to be sure that I can continue to be a writer without being branded by the malice of people who make a living by that malice. I also want to go on saying that I am a Jew without being afraid that I will be called names or end in a prison camp." One of her finest plays, "The Watch on the Rhine" was a severe indictment of that evil period of history.

"The Little Foxes," and "Another Part of the Forest" as well as her adaptation of "The Lark" have added more honors to her career. Many of her plays have become fine motion pictures.

Now successful and wealthy, the hardworking and resourceful Lillian Hellman has gone beyond the point where she could be considered America's greatest woman playwright. She is now perhaps the greatest writer for the theatre regardless of sex.

Theodore
HERZL

Father Of Political Zionism

In the year 70, a Roman army overran Palestine, destroyed the Second Temple, and sacked Jerusalem. From that time, Jews all over the world prayed every day for the recovery of their homeland. In 1897—over 18 centuries later—Jews from all corners of the earth met in Basle, Switzerland, and proclaimed their right to live their own lives in the land of their forefathers, Palestine.

This meeting in Basle was the first Zionist Congress, and the man who was responsible for its convening was Theodor Herzl.

Born in Budapest in 1860, Herzl was educated in Vienna. At 20, he was a celebrated playwright and journalist. Sent to Paris to cover the infamous Dreyfus trial, Herzl was shocked and alarmed to note the ugly anti-Semitism rampant in the civilized world. From then on, his goal was to emancipate his scattered people and find them a home they could call their own.

As leader of the Zionist organization, Herzl was acclaimed as a savior by millions of Jews all over the world. For 8 years, he devoted his entire energies and his talents as a writer, orator and politician to achieving his desire and that of his people. He pleaded the cause of the Jews before sultans and kings, ministers, financiers, even the Pope in Rome. Everywhere he met failure.

As the bloody massacres of the Jews continued all over Europe, the desperate Herzl even offered to accept a British colony in East Africa as a haven for his people. To him, a home anywhere was more urgent than Palestine. But the masses of the Jews turned against Herzl's proposal. Even his closest followers began to desert him.

Despondent, weary and ill, Theodor Herzl, the father of political Zionism, died in 1904 while in the prime of his life. He was buried in Vienna. But the fire he had kindled in the hearts of Jews burned on, as bright and insistent as ever. Zionism struggled against odds for many more years until, at last, the goal was finally reached and Israel again became a nation. A year later, Herzl's body was taken from the Vienna cemetery and flown to Israel. It was borne through the streets of Tel Aviv as 250,000 Jews reverently marched in the funeral procession. He was reburied near Jerusalem on a hill now called Mount Herzl.

Today he looks down on Israel from his mountaintop, on the Promised Land that came into being because of his early, heroic efforts to bring it to realization. For as he once said, "I believe we have given something to the Jewish people—to the young, a hope—to the old, a dream—to all men, something beautiful."

Myra HESS

The Grand Dame Of The Keyboard

Myra Hess was born in Hampstead, England, in 1890. Her family was orthodox and she was taught Hebrew as a child. At the same time, she began the study of the piano, and almost immediately it became obvious that the little girl was destined to make her mark as a musician. She made her professional debut at 17. Her playing created a sensation, and she was promptly engaged to appear as solo pianist with the famed London Philharmonic.

When her reputation in England and Europe was soundly established, she came for the first time to America. Her first appearance there in 1922 was acclaimed by both press and public. Myra Hess won praise not only as a fine pianist but also as a true virtuoso, regardless of sex.

As the years passed, the popularity and fame of Myra Hess became more and more solidly established. In 1939, she was again giving concerts in America when, suddenly, World War II began. She returned at once to England to take her place with her countrymen in their hour of danger.

In London, Myra Hess began a series of daily concerts at the National Gallery. Every day at noon, in spite of air attacks, buzz bombs and danger of invasion, the great pianist calmly sat down to play. Sometimes it was impossible for her audience—civilians, wounded veterans, soldiers, officers, young and old—to make their way to the concert hall through the destruction in the streets. But the concerts went on, day after day, without interruption.

By the end of the war, Myra Hess had given 1,698 concerts before a total audience of more than a million listeners. A grateful sovereign, mindful of the tremendous lift to morale given the British people by Myra Hess in the darkest hours of the war, conferred on her the highest honor that could be bestowed on a woman. King George VI made her a Dame Commander of the British Empire. Thereafter, as Dame Myra Hess, she continued to give concerts as the supreme artist of the keyboard and the only woman pianist ever to have been knighted.

Nat
HOLMAN

Mr. Basketball

He was an obscure skinny Jewish boy from the sidewalks of New York with a fantastic dream to win fame as a basketball player. In that fabulous Golden Age of Sports during the Roaring Twenties, an era from which emerged history's most immortal champions, Nat Holman made his boyhood dream come true. For he became the most famous, the highest-paid, and the greatest basketball player in the world. The most brilliant star of the legendary Original Celtics, the greatest professional basketball team of all time, Holman won the acclaim of historians and fans as the most scientific and the greatest basketball player in history.

At the height of his fame as a living basketball immortal, Holman also became the basketball coach at the College of the City of New York. And he enriched that famed institution of higher learning with a world-wide basketball fame.

The little gymnasium on that college campus became Holman's world. There, he taught basketball to poor boys from the grubby sidewalks and teeming tenements of New York who came to City College for free book learning. Most of them were no athletes who came to "The Master" to learn basketball, but Holman performed magic feats as a basketball coach. He developed famous basketball players out of fine students and book-worms. Holman's teams won national fame, and they were always among the very best in the game. He became the most famous basketball coach in America.

He was more than just a basketball coach. He was also a teacher, and an authoritative lucid lecturer and fine writer on the science of the game. Universally, he came to be known as "Mr. Basketball."

As the dean of all basketball coaches, it was in 1950 when he climaxed his many years of basketball glory by achieving a distinction as is not often the lot of any man. For that season, he produced a C.C.N.Y. "wonder five" that scored an unprecedented sweep of the two major national basketball tournaments. It was the first and only time in history that a college team ever won both of those coveted basketball championships, in a single season.

Nat Holman remained basketball coach at City College for 36 years. Many honors came to him as Jewry's greatest basketball idol, not the least of which was an invitation to come to Israel and introduce the game of basketball to this new nation, and teach basketball to its youth.

Vladimir
HOROWITZ

There Is Only One

On January 12, 1928, Vladimir Horowitz made his American debut with the New York Philharmonic Orchestra. The American audience, not easily stirred by unknown musicians, went wild over him. No pianist ever created a greater furore in the music world.

Behind that debut were many years of the hardest, most intense work. As a boy in Kiev, Horowitz began to play when he was 6. He was encouraged by his mother, herself a gifted pianist. He was enrolled in the Kiev Conservatory when he was 12. At 17, he graduated with the highest honors.

The following year, his uncle, a music critic, arranged the boy's first official concert in Kharkov. Horowitz, who was barely 18, was a sensation. For days on end, the city buzzed with excitement about the new piano virtuoso. Horowitz had to give 13 concerts in Kharkov before they would let him go. He went on to give 70 concerts all over Russia, playing a different program for each—a total of 200 compositions in all.

There followed a triumphant tour of Europe and then the sensational American debut. His fees for playing soared from $500 a concert to $1,500. He fulfilled hundreds of engagements. And then, suddenly, Vladimir Horowitz withdrew from the concert hall. For two years nothing was heard from him. Dissatisfied with what he was accomplishing, Horowitz did nothing but rest and study and reflect. He did not touch a piano keyboard. Then, out of that period of hibernation, there came forth a new Horowitz, a pianist who had added soul and emotion to the greatest technique known. In 1939, he returned to the concert stage. Again the world acclaimed him as the greatest pianist of them all. His fees rose to $5,000 a performance, and his appearances were limited only by his own wishes. From that day, Horowitz ranked as one of the immortals of the keyboard, a pianist whose technique and intensity of temperament could combine to raise an audience to a higher state of excitement and exhilaration than any other pianist in the world.

Harry
HOUDINI

The Magician Who Baffled A World

Although Houdini has been dead for some years, his name has become a part of the English language. "To do a Houdini" is to slip out of a tight situation. The feats by which Houdini made himself a household word were the most amazing, the most mystifying, ever seen on or off the stage.

Born as Ehrich Weiss in Appleton, Wisconsin, in 1874, Harry Houdini was the son of a poor rabbi. He saw his first circus performance when he was only 7. When he saw a magician perform his tricks, his life work was decided. Houdini went home and immediately began to practice acrobatics and rope-walking. He devoured books of magic while working as a newsboy to help out his father.

Apprenticed early to a locksmith, Houdini made a study of locks that was to prove of inestimable value to him in later life. He continued to study and practice tricks. Ready for the stage, he took the name of Houdini and began to present himself in an act of magic tricks, card manipulations and handcuff escapes. He worked in dime museums, beer halls, circuses and carnivals.

Little by little, his reputation grew. Soon he was astounding audiences with his remarkable escape from a straitjacket. And when he first performed his feat of escaping from handcuffs and iron chains, Houdini was acknowledged the world's most famous artist of mystification and magic.

Houdini continued to develop his great escape feats. Some of the most spectacular of them remain as the most memorable tricks ever seen. Among them were his escapes from prison cells in which he had been handcuffed and fettered. On other occasions, he permitted himself to be bound hand and foot and locked inside a heavy chest which was lowered to the bottom of a river. In a few minutes, he would appear at the surface, free of his bonds, and none the worse for the experience.

When Harry Houdini died, he took most of his amazing escape secrets to the grave with him. They have never been revealed or duplicated to this day. In his own field of magic and sleight-of-hand, Houdini was the greatest of them all.

Sol HUROK

The Impresario

When he was only 14, Sol Hurok was considered shrewd enough by his father, a hardware merchant in the little town of Pogar, Russia, to go out on buying trips alone. On these trips, the boy saw Russia's big cities and soon Pogar became too small for him. His father gave him some money to go to Kharkov to set himself up as a hardware merchant. The next thing that happened was a long, illegal trip by steerage to far-off America.

The year was 1906. Hurok became a peddler, then a factory worker, street-car conductor, hardware salesman. Life looked good when his salary rose to $7 a week. But one night Hurok went to a concert by the great Chaliapin. Far up in the gallery, the young man was overcome by the beauty of Chaliapin's voice. He rushed home to write a letter to the great Russian artist, offering to become his manager. There was no reply.

In time, Hurok began to stage concerts and benefits at the Labor Lyceum in Brooklyn's teeming Jewish neighborhood of Brownsville. So successful were they that he founded a musical society for the presentation of concert artists. Again he had great success with his offerings. Again he wrote Chaliapin in Paris, renewing his offer. This time he received a cable in reply. "Meet me in Paris. Chaliapin."

Hurok scraped together what money he had and took the next boat. In Paris, Chaliapin looked at him and laughed. "So you're the one," he said. "I just wanted to see what you looked like."

Hurok returned home broke. He threw himself into the career of an impresario, determined to bring culture and art to the people. He rented the Hippodrome, once New York's largest theatre, for a series of Sunday concerts, offering the greatest names in music, at only two dollars a ticket. The masses came in droves. The artists who saw this hungry surge for culture, responded with enthusiasm. The most famous signed to perform for Sol Hurok. And, eventually, even the great Chaliapin too came to sing for the little impresario.

"Sol Hurok Presents" became a byword in the musical world and the theatre. Every great artist, singer, dancer, choir, ballet and theatre group in the world—all have been brought to America to appear under Hurok's auspices. He became so famous an impresario that Hollywood filmed a motion picture of his life to tell his fantastic success story to the world.

American audiences can be eternally grateful to Sol Hurok from the Old World for his unquenchable urge to bring culture and art to the New World.

AL JOLSON

The Jazz Singer

Famous as he was as a popular singer for the masses, Al Jolson will always be remembered as the first star of the talking motion picture. When the experiment of changing from silent films to sound was considered, the Warner Brothers wanted the strongest star of film and stage to lead the way. And Al Jolson, one of the greatest names in the theatre, was chosen to make the plunge. His first talking picture, "The Jazz Singer," revolutionized the industry and brought talkies to every screen all over the world.

Born Asa Yoelson in St. Petersburg, Russia, in 1886, Jolson was the son of a poor cantor who himself represented the sixth in a direct line who had been cantors. It was the father's hope that his son would follow in his footsteps and become a cantor too. But when he brought the 7-year-old Al to America, the boy took to singing in the streets, and his taste seemed to lean to ragtime. The stage drew him like a magnet. He got into vaudeville with the famous Dockstader minstrels, and achieved fame as a blackface artist of song. He was brought to Broadway by the Shuberts, and leaped to stardom in a series of Winter Garden musical hit shows. It was after starring in many of these that Hollywood called on him to make the historic first talking picture.

From the stage and films, Jolson went on to great fame in radio as well. His voice, with its characteristic richness of sound, his own special style and manner, made him a popular and beloved performer, recognized instantly everywhere. He was probably the most imitated singer and artist in the theatre.

When Al Jolson died in 1950, more than 20,000 mourners attended his funeral. He left behind him a fortune of several million dollars, more than nine-tenths of which was willed by him to charity.

Albert
KAHN

Architect For The World

Thousands of buildings all over the world today stand as mute monuments to the genius of Albert Kahn, creator of a new industrial architecture and father of the modern daylight factory.

Albert Kahn was the son of an impoverished rabbi in Germany. Brought to America at 12, he found a job as office boy in an architect's office. He studied drawing in his spare time and won a $500 scholarship and an opportunity to study architecture in Europe. On returning to America, he started to practice. His early years as an architect were fantastically ill-rewarded, but in 1903 he finally landed the job of designing a new engineering building for the University of Michigan. It was his biggest assignment after 12 lean years and it started him on his way to fame.

A year later, Kahn designed and built a factory for the Packard Motor Company. A daring departure in design, it was the first reinforced concrete factory in America and the first in which windows were adequate and departments were coordinated for efficiency. Quickly, Kahn became America's outstanding authority on concrete factory design and a pioneer in combining utility with dignity and beauty. He built factories for General Motors, Hudson, Republic Steel, Ford, Chrysler, and innumerable others. His greatest job was Willow Run (now Ford's), built originally as a bomber plant and the largest single building ever erected at one time.

He designed millions of dollars worth of construction for the Army. The heavy construction program of the Soviet Union's first five year plan was entrusted to him, a two-billion-dollar task. He built industrial plants and factories in England, France, Sweden, Japan. By 1939, Albert Kahn had designed and built on every one of the five continents of the world.

At Kahn's death in 1942, his office was handling more factory construction than any other industrial architect in the world. Kahn applied the mass production ideas of industry to the art of architecture, sometimes building as many as 40 structures at a time with the help of his 650-man staff. He himself worked almost to his dying day, planning and designing the most beautiful and most useful structures in the world.

DANNY
KAYE

Everybody's Clown

On a slum street in the teeming Brownsville section of Brooklyn, New York, that spawned many hoodlums several who were destined to win notoriety by dying in the electric chair, Danny Kominski was born in 1913. He was to win world fame as Danny Kaye.

Son of a poor dress designer, his childhood was hard. Rent was always a problem in his home, and enough food was always a luxury. Still, Danny grew up with laughter and song in his heart. When he was only 10, he could convulse street corner audiences by making funny faces and singing strange little songs.

Schooling didn't interest him much, and before he could finish high school, he ran away to Florida—to be an entertainer. He left with only seventy-five cents in his pocket. However, he earned his way by singing songs to a friend's guitar accompaniment.

Finally, Danny Kominski returned home and he decided to settle down. He took a job as a clerk for an insurance company. But after only 18 months, he was fired for being a nitwit. He had made one mistake that cost the company a loss of $40,000.

So, Danny Kominski turned his back on a business career, changed his name to Danny Kaye, and he began to entertain at summer resorts in the Catskill Mountains. From $200 a season, he worked himself up to $1,000 a season. During the winters he lived on his summer earnings while tramping Broadway searching for a stage job. Finally, after four years of frus-

tration, he joined a vaudeville act. He was no howling success. But one evening while trying to kiss the pretty girl in his stage act, he accidentally fell flat on his face. The audience howled with laughter. So, Danny Kaye became a clown.

The day came at last when he found himself on Broadway, in a stage revue. His debut as a comedian in the big time of show business was sensational. His satirical antics and clever songs (written mostly by his wife, a girl from his old Brownsville neighborhood) brought him the widest and warmest acclaim from the critics, swank society and the masses. One stage hit followed another. Soon, his charm and humor also conquered motion pictures, and his fame as a clown became universal.

Traveling countless miles throughout Europe, Africa, the Orient, the Mediterranean, the Near East, Palestine, and everywhere else, the children of the world fell in love with Danny Kaye. His funny face and his happy rollicking antics was his passport to their hearts. To the children of the world, regardless of nationality, race or color, Danny Kaye became their modern Pied Piper to lead them to laughter and happiness. The grownups also took him to their hearts. He became a particular favorite of the Queen of England, and royalty fawned upon him. He has earned a fabulous fortune as a comedian.

Today, Danny Kaye, once a boy without a future in a Brownsville slum, is the most famous and the most beloved clown in the world!

Serge
KOUSSEVITZKY

Man With A Baton

Serge Koussevitzky knew from his earliest childhood that he wanted to be a conductor when he grew up. Barely able to toddle, he would line up two rows of chairs, then stand before them waving a baton. His father, a professional musician, gave the boy his first music lessons and discovered that he had unusual talent. When he was 7, Serge had his first experience as a conductor—conducting his own compositions. He joined the string section of an orchestra when he was only 9, and two years later, at 11, he was serving as substitute for the permanent conductor. At 14, he was a full-fledged regular conductor of an orchestra.

Koussevitzky became a famous concert artist on the double bass, that enormous instrument which no one believed could be used alone to make music. He developed such technique in using the double bass that he amazed the music world. He could have gone on to be a great virtuoso and teacher, but such a life was not for him. His childhood dream still haunted him. When his wealthy father-in-law asked him in 1905 what he wanted for a wedding gift,

Koussevitzky had but one reply—a symphony orchestra! And an orchestra he received!

Koussevitzky went on from triumph to triumph as an orchestra conductor, and came to America in 1924 at the invitation of Boston music-lovers to revive the one-time fine Boston Symphony which had been founded in 1881. With this organization, Koussevitzky became one of the greatest masters of conducting technique, and the Boston Symphony became famous the world over under his guidance.

Koussevitzky's magnetic personality restored glamour to the art of conducting, and his dynamic leadership made Boston one of the great centers of music-making in the world. For 25 years, he led the orchestra, and when he passed the baton on to younger hands in 1948, it was considered one of the finest in the world.

In 1940, another of his life-long dreams was realized when he founded the Berkshire Music Center where students, teachers and professional musicians could gather, teach and study and exchange experiences and ideas. The Tanglewood concerts at the center remain as a memorial to his great talents in music.

Wanda
LANDOWSKA

The Genius Of The Harpsichord

No woman ever commanded a more imposing position in modern musical history than Wanda Landowska, genius of the harpsichord. Trained from girlhood as pianist and composer, she found, in her native Poland, that music seemed to begin and end with Chopin, the national god. Nothing written before his day seemed to exist either for the interpreters of music or the conservatories.

Wanda tried to rebel against the narrow teachings of her instructors. It was not till her family, part of Warsaw's upper Jewish bourgeoisie, sent her to the Warsaw Conservatory that she was able to experiment a little with the older composers like Bach. When she was 14, she gave her first concert in Warsaw. Meanwhile, her voice training was receiving almost as much attention as her piano-playing. At 17, when she was sent to Berlin, then the Mecca of all music, to continue her studies, she turned to composing and singing. She was getting nowhere musically when suddenly she fell in love with a compatriot who was an ardent Zionist. They married and went to Paris. There she met a brilliant group of musicians. Her entire attitude changed. She began to explore pre-19th century music and its interpretation. And she came to the conclusion that Bach and his predecessors could not be played properly on the piano.

Looking around her, her eye fell on a long-unused instrument called the harpsichord. She began to experiment with it, improved it, played on it. Little by little, beginning in 1903, she added to her concerts pieces played on the harpsichord. Her friends tried to dissuade her from using the archaic and imperfect instrument, as they called it. But Wanda Landowska persisted. She perfected her style, widened her repertory, forged a new technique for the playing of this instrument, and she taught the world to accept the harpsichord. She scored fantastic triumphs on concert tours thruout Europe and America, and everywhere she was hailed for her genius with the harpsichord. A "Landowska cult" spread across the musical world, and students from all over the globe came to her to learn and to study the playing of this ancient instrument. They went back out into the world to perform on their own as harpsichordists, and the proudest designation each bore for musical recognition was to be known as a "Wanda Landowska student."

At the age of 70, the world's greatest harpsichordist, grown into a living musical immortal, devoted all her energies to record the gigantic composition of "The Well-Tempered Clavier." She called it "my last will and testament."

[71]

Emma
LAZARUS

The Statue Of Liberty Is Her Monument

Emma Lazarus, daughter of a wealthy Portuguese Jew, grew up in New York City with little real love or admiration for her people. As a young poet, she came under the influence of Ralph Waldo Emerson, great American essayist and poet, who admired her work but reproved her for her cold intellectual approach and lack of Jewish traditional influence.

Brooding over the criticism, Emma Lazarus took to visiting Ellis Island to watch the arrival of the pathetic refugees who were then, in 1881 and 1882, fleeing the terrible pogroms of Russia to freedom in America. Deeply stirred by the pitiful sight of her co-religionists in flight from misery and oppression, her writing began to be animated with fiery concern for the Jewish people.

She studied her religion and the history of her people. She learned Hebrew so that she could translate some of the great Jewish poetry. And she wrote new poems that were filled with love for her own faith and people. One of those poems has become world-famous, both for its content and the use to which it was put. The poem, called "The New Colossus," describes once and for all what she felt about the refugees she had seen at Ellis Island. In part it said:

". . . Give me your tired, your poor,
Your huddled masses yearning to breathe free,
The wretched refuse of your teeming shore,
Send these, the homeless, tempest-tossed, to me,
I lift my lamp beside the golden door!"

The lines were inscribed on a brass tablet fitted into the base of the Statue of Liberty which stands in New York Harbor and welcomes the newcomer to these shores. Millions have read them and more will read them in the years to come. They stand as a fitting memorial to Emma Lazarus, who learned to love her people and the teeming masses of humanity who fled the Old World to find a haven in the New.

Death struck her down in the full bloom of life. She was only 38 when she died, in 1891. Her tombstone stands in a Long Island graveyard, and a public memorial to her was put up in her native New York City.

Herbert
LEHMAN

The Conscience Of The Senate

No Jew in political life has brought more honor to his people than Herbert Lehman, first of his faith to be elected to the United States Senate by popular vote. Other Jews who had served in the upper house of Congress before him had been either appointed or elected by state legislatures, a procedure changed by the 17th Amendment to the Constitution to direct elections.

Herbert Lehman, who was born in New York in 1878, had been raised in luxury as the son of a German immigrant who had founded the famous investment firm of Lehman Brothers and co-founded the New York Cotton Exchange. In spite of his background of wealth and affluence, young Lehman was to devote all his energy and time to aiding the lowly and the humble. No one would ever speak with greater earnestness for the rights of man and social justice.

After completing his college course, Herbert Lehman entered welfare work with the famed Henry Street Settlement. He entered the family banking business after a short time in the textile field. Then, in 1913, he became a member of a commission to revise the banking laws of New York. So able did he prove that he

was prevailed on to enter politics. He won his first elective office as lieutenant-governor of New York in 1928, as the running mate of F. D. Roosevelt. Later, when Roosevelt went on to the White House, Lehman stepped into the Governor's chair himself. He won national recognition as an official of spirit, force, power and intelligence. He was elected governor four times and served in that high office for ten years, longer than any man in history.

The length of his service in the Governor's mansion was less notable than the extraordinary record he made there in the field of social reform, particularly laws regarding social and religious discrimination, labor reform and protection of the aged and youth.

In 1942, he resigned the governorship to become President Roosevelt's Director-General of the United Nations Relief and Rehabilitation Administration. In 1949, he went to Washington as Senator from New York. There he served as the conscience of the Senate and America's stoutest champion of civil rights and anti-discrimination. Truly has Herbert Lehman been called a saint among men and an outstanding example of honesty, integrity and courage in politics. Few men in American history have had such a distinguished career in government.

Benny LEONARD

A Legend Of The Prize-Ring

Born in poverty, bred in the obscurity of New York's teeming lower East Side, Benjamin Leiner, the son of a humble orthodox family, became under the name of Leonard, the greatest and the most famous Jewish sport champion in history. He was the first Jew in America to win universal fame as a sports idol, as well as the complete love of his own people.

Against his parents' wishes, he became a prizefighter at 16, for he wanted to earn some money and better their hard lot in life. Before he passed his 21st birthday, he was the lightweight champion of the world. His reign as a titleholder lasted 8 years, the longest in history, and he was never defeated as a lightweight champion. He left behind him such an unmatched ring record that it has become accepted by all that Leonard was the greatest lightweight champion in history, and perhaps the cleverest boxing master ever known to the prize-ring.

A model son, he was ringdom's original "Mama's Boy," for wherever he went to fight he carried his mother's picture with him, and always after a fight he phoned her to assure her that all was well with him. His devotion to his mother was genuine. He was also an observing Jew. He never fought on a Jewish holiday. And as an idol of the Jewish people, he took his role seriously. He took an active part in Zionist affairs and in Jewish community life, and always he was aware of the problems facing Jewry. It was said that Benny Leonard as a ring champion did more with his fists to destroy anti-Semitism than any Jew of his time.

For his first ring bout, he received less than ten dollars. Before he finished with prizefighting, he had earned more than a million dollars. But more than that, he earned the universal respect of all Jews. He became the most admired and best loved sport champion Jewry ever had.

After his fighting days in the ring, Leonard became a boxing referee. For he said: "Boxing has been my life. I will be in it until I breathe my last."

He was. For on the night of April 18, 1947, while refereeing a bout, he collapsed and died—in the ring. He was only 51. It was a strange end for the greatest Jewish name in sports history.

In Israel, there now stands a fitting monument to the memory of Benny Leonard. It is a huge building devoted to the science of boxing. It is called, "The Benny Leonard Arena."

Judge
SAMUEL
LEIBOWITZ

A Courtroom For His Fame

During the first half of the 20th century, Samuel Leibowitz was America's most spectacular criminal lawyer. He achieved an almost legendary fame as one of the most successful criminal lawyers of all time. For in many of the most sensational murder trials of this century, as the attorney for the defense, he compiled an amazing record of acquittals. He saved all but one of his 140 defendants from execution in the electric chair.

The case that stamped his fame with international acclaim as a "genius of the courtroom" was winning the release of the Scottsboro Boys —nine young Negroes who had been condemned to death sentences. It was a celebrated case of Southern injustice which for years had created bitter controversy throughout the world. As a matter of principle, Samuel Leibowitz refused to accept any fee for the spectacular part he played as chief defense counsel in that memorable case of justice for the innocent.

He was born in Roumania in 1893, under the name of Samuel Lebeau. He was brought to the United States at the age of four, to live in a dingy tenement house on New York's lower East Side. His father, Isaac Lebeau, the owner of a small drygoods store was persuaded by his Jewish neighbors to Americanize his name, so that his son might have a better chance for success in the New World. So, the name of Lebeau was changed to Leibowitz.

Urged by his father to study law, Samuel Leibowitz worked his way through college and he earned his law degree at Cornell University. At the age of 24, he was admitted to practice at the New York bar. He began as a clerk with a civil law firm, at $35 a week. But he soon became bored with such dull work, and he turned to criminal law. Young and unknown, to get clients, he offered his services for free to penniless defendants. He gained the reputation of a lawyer who could not lose a case. Before long, Samuel Leibowitz became the most noted criminal lawyer in the world's largest city. On all sides, his services were now in demand at high fees. But, as a man of principle, he often refused many cases which were offered him. On one occasion, he refused a tempting fee of $200,000 to defend a notorious gangster.

In 1941, at the age of only 47, when he was at the height of his fame and success as America's greatest criminal lawyer, Samuel Leibowitz suddenly decided to give up his turbulent life in a courtroom, and seek the quiet life and solemn dignity of an honored judge. He was elected to sit on the bench of the Kings County Court, the highest criminal court in New York State.

At the end of 1956, he was still an honored and respected judge, rendering decisions and judgments as spectacularly outstanding as were the pleas he used to make defending the innocent when he stood in a courtroom in his full fame as America's most spectacular criminal lawyer.

Uriah
Phillips
LEVY

A Sailor For History

Like so many other naval heroes, Uriah Levy ran away from home as a boy of 10 to follow the sea. He was a cabin boy at 11, and advanced through the ranks until, at 20, he was the captain and part owner of a schooner. His life as a sailor and master was full of adventure. In 1812, his own crew mutinied and seized his ship and cargo, leaving him to die on a deserted island. But Levy was rescued and he pursued the piratical crew to the West Indies and brought them back to Boston for trial and punishment for their acts.

During the War of 1812, Levy became a sailing master in the fledgling United States Navy and helped capture several British vessels. As commander of one of the captured ships, Levy roamed the high seas in search of the enemy. He was himself captured by the British and taken to England. After six months, he was released and returned to America where a grateful government, remembering what he had done in the war, promoted him to lieutenant.

Uriah Levy spent the next forty years in the United States Navy, but the time was filled with much strife and bitterness for him. Many of the other officers of the line resented him, both for the promotions he earned so gallantly, and the fact that he was a Jew. Levy fought several duels, common in the Navy at the time, and on one occasion killed his opponent. Always bitter about the treatment of ordinary seamen who were flogged brutally for their transgressions, however trivial, he fought hard to have the cruel punishment stopped. He finally succeeded in getting a law passed abolishing forever all corporal punishment in the United States Navy.

The opposition of his fellow-officers in the Navy grew more and more bitter as Levy rose in rank. He was forced to defend himself against unjust court-martials from time to time, and once President Monroe himself intervened to save him from being expelled from the service. But nevertheless, Uriah Levy at last reached a height which no Jewish officer had ever before attained. He was appointed Commodore, highest rank in the service at that time. It was a fitting reward for a gallant and devoted officer who had given his life to the service of his country.

David LUBIN

A Friend To The Farmers Of The World

The career of David Lubin was one of the most unique ever followed by an American immigrant. Born of orthodox parents in Klodowa, Galicia, Lubin was brought to America as a child and settled on New York's East Side. After the Civil War, Lubin traveled west and prospected for gold in Arizona. After various occupations, he finally opened a general store in Sacramento in 1874. There he put into operation a number of innovations that establish Lubin as one of America's merchandising pioneers.

The store, which was above a saloon, bore a sign which said, DAVID LUBIN—ONE-PRICE STORE. The idea of fixed prices was thus put into use for the first time. Other new ideas conceived by Lubin were to mark all merchandise clearly with its selling price and a rigid adherence to truth in representing goods or articles.

The people of Sacramento flocked to this unusual store where there was no haggling and no misrepresentation. Soon Lubin opened another store in San Francisco, again breaking ground in merchandising methods. He had founded the first chain of stores in America.

Lubin might have continued being a merchant had he not made a trip to Palestine in 1884. There he grew interested in farming and when he returned to the United States, he began to study soils and methods by which the best products could be raised. He became the owner of the largest fruit-packing company in California.

Lubin was convinced that the consumer could buy more and better food at lower prices if there was world-wide cooperation among farmers. He founded the International Institute for Agriculture. Through this organization, Lubin convinced nation after nation of the value of his idea of pooling knowledge to improve the food of the world. Forty-five countries joined his plan and made up the first permanent international cooperative organization in the world. The Institute met in Rome and the King of Italy gave it a beautiful building for its use. Farmers from all parts of the globe were sent by their countries to talk with each other about their problems and exchange information about soil and crops.

David Lubin died in Rome in 1919, mourned the world over as "The Farmers' Friend."

Judah
MACCABEE

The Festival Of Lights Shine For Him

One of five sons of the aged priest, Mattathias, who had himself challenged the powerful authority of Antiochus, the Syrian King, Judah Maccabee was one of history's most essential heroes. Had it not been for him, it is likely that neither Judaism nor Christianity would have come down to us as living faiths. For the Jews were close to extermination as Jews in the year 165 B.C.E. Unwilling to see his religion or his people die, Judah Maccabee took arms against pagan oppression that had already succeeded in desecrating the Temple in Jerusalem and frightening many Jews away from their faith. Some, it is true, had been willing to die rather than give in. But many had succumbed to the Syrian threats and cruelty. In one way or another, Judaism would have been crushed under the brutal force of idolatry and paganism, had it not been for this brave and heroic military genius.

At the beginning of 165 B.C.E., the Temple had been desecrated by Antiochus's Syrian soldiers. The Law had been abolished on pain of death. The Jews had been coerced into a pagan way of life when Judah the Maccabee (Hammer) rose with a small band of dedicated soldiers to make war against the tyranny of Antiochus. A guerrilla fighter, first among the Jews, he was considered little more than a robber by the tyrant. But to his own people whose faith and freedom he set out to restore, he was a savior. He won battle after battle with his small band against the trained armies of the Syrians. Finally, at Emmaus, Judah Maccabee led an army of 3,000 to a tremendous victory over 50,000 Syrians. And, at last, he reentered the Holy City of Jerusalem.

First he destroyed the idols of the defeated Syrians. Then he reconsecrated the Temple and declared a festival to commemorate the occasion, the first ever instituted by human hand in the history of Israel. This took place on the 25th day of Kislev (December), and the rededication of the purified altar was celebrated for eight days. This celebration is held with joy and gladness every year at the same time since that first dedication, and it is called Hannukah.

Judah L. MAGNES

A University For His Monument

The Hebrew University on Mount Scopus in Jerusalem holds a commanding position in the sphere of learning everywhere. No man is more closely identified with this famed institution which was wholly planned and perfected by Jews, than Judah L. Magnes, an American.

He was born in San Francisco, California, in 1877. At 21, he graduated from the University of Cincinnati, and two years later, he received his rabbinical degree from the Hebrew Union College. In 1902, he left the University of Heidelberg with the degree of Doctor of Philosophy.

Upon his return to the United States, Doctor Magnes entered the active rabbinate, and in 1908, he accepted the influential pulpit of Temple Emanu-El in New York. Fervently preaching and advocating a rededication of the true spirit of Judaism and a return to its sacred traditions, Rabbi Magnes soon resigned from the leadership of that important congregation to become the spiritual leader of the oldest orthodox congregation in New York. But a year later, he decided to leave the active rabbinate entirely. He became the leader of the Society for Advancement of Judaism. Throwing himself wholeheartedly into this movement, he organized "The Kehillah" which profoundly influenced all community organizations for Jewish education throughout the United States. Into "The Kehillah" he brought together all the diverse groups, temples, synagogues, schools, lodges, labor unions, social clubs and Zionist organizations. He also helped found the Yiddish daily newspaper "Der Tag" and he sponsored the Intercollegiate Menorah Society.

Judah Magnes became an ardent Zionist, and because he raised his brilliant oratorical voice in defense of Jews everywhere, he became known as "Magnes—the Universalist!" In 1916, he headed the first commission that went to Europe to arrange for the distribution of American Jewish relief funds.

With the end of World War I, he undertook the organization of the new Hebrew University in Jerusalem. He withdrew to Palestine there to live, work, plan and perfect that vast project. He secured the initial funds for the construction of this Hebrew University, and the endowments for its maintenance. He laid the basis for its academic structure. In 1925, when the Hebrew University opened, Dr. Magnes became its first Chancellor.

His was an inspiring service to this university during its first difficult years. He labored hard to recreate in the Holy Land a Jewish cultural renaissance. In 1935, he became the President of the Hebrew University.

Honored in many lands, always he remained a controversial figure in Palestine, as often he clashed with the majority political opinion. He spent his last years laboring in a vain effort to bring about unity and peace among the Jews and Arabs. He died in 1949.

Always the Hebrew University in Jerusalem will stand as a monument to his fame and place in Jewish history.

Moses
MAIMONIDES

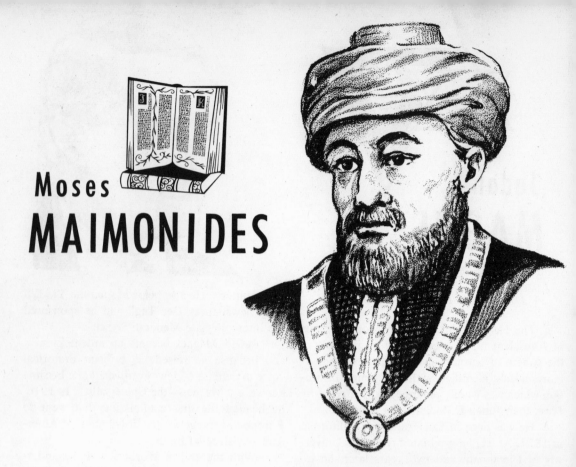

The First Physician

Moses Maimonides, great genius of Judaism in the Middle Ages, was born on Passover Eve, 1135, in Cordova, Spain. Originally known as Moses ben Maimon, he was a member of a family noted for its scholars and its piety. When he was only 12, Spain was overrun by the Mohammedans, and he and his family were forced to flee for their lives. After much wandering in Spain, under the pretense of being themselves Mohammedans, they settled in Cairo, Egypt. There the boy, already possessed of great intellectual gifts, became a rabbi like his fathers before him. But to earn a living, he studied medicine and became a physician and surgeon.

Maimonides soon became famous, both for his learning and for his skill in medicine. The outstanding scholar of his time, he was consulted far and wide on the most abstruse questions of philosophy and religion. As a physician, he attained the very highest rank and became court physician to the Sultan Saladin.

It is said that during the Crusades, Maimonides was called on to save the life of the English King Richard when he was wounded near Jerusalem.

As philosopher, astronomer and Talmudist, Maimonides towered above all the scholars in the world of the Middle Ages. When 52, he completed the "Moreh Nebuchim," or "Guide for the Perplexed." And after 30 years of work, he prepared the "Mishnah Torah."

Because of his great fame and his good works, the Jews during most of his lifetime lived free of persecution. Maimonides was a man of such deep piety that he has often been compared with the first Moses, the man of God.

The world-famous healer of body and soul died before his 70th year and was buried in Tiberias, Israel, where his tomb now stands. The world's first great Jewish physician whose life had been devoted to good works left behind him a tradition and a heritage which will always be a source of great hope and courage to his people.

Col. David (Mickey) MARCUS

Israel's Secret Warrior

The son of a Roumanian immigrant, David "Mickey" Marcus was raised in the teeming Jewish section of Brooklyn, New York, known as Brownsville. A fine athlete and student in high school, Mickey went on to West Point and graduated in 1924. He studied law, and in 1933 was appointed Acting Commissioner of Correction in charge of New York City's prison system.

When World War II broke out, Marcus was drawn back into military service as lieutenant-colonel and attached to the Chief of Staff, General George C. Marshall. Among other actions in which he was involved, Marcus went into Normandy with the airborne troops. He was chosen to accompany President Roosevelt at the historic conferences of Yalta and Teheran, and later with President Truman at the Potsdam meeting. In the closing weeks of the war, he helped draw up surrender documents for Italy and Germany as well as the program for occupied areas.

By the end of the war, Mickey Marcus was a full colonel. After short service with General MacArthur in the Pacific, he came home to resume his law practice. On his tunic he wore the coveted ribbons of the Distinguished Service Cross and the Bronze Star for gallantry.

But Colonel Mickey Marcus had not finished with military matters. Another career, and, as a Jew, a more important one, still lay before him. The Jewish Agency interested him in the cause of liberating Palestine. He was smuggled into the Holy Land where he set up the first military manuals ever published in Hebrew. He organized officers' training schools and secretly trained the Haganah and instructed them on the types of guns and ammunition to purchase. He returned to Brooklyn, his work seemingly finished. But in 1948, when the Israeli War of Independence began, Mickey Marcus was back in Israel in command of its troops. Just a few hours before the cease-fire ended the war, on June 11, 1948, Colonel David "Mickey" Marcus was killed in action while leading Haganah troops on the Jerusalem front.

His body was brought back to America. The hero of two wars and two worlds was laid to rest in West Point's historic cemetery.

Alicia
MARKOVA

Immortal Ballerina

There were four girls in the Marks family in London, and the smallest, daintiest and frailest of them all was the eldest, Lillian Alicia. The family doctor suggested that dancing lessons might help build up the fragile little girl. Her mother enrolled her in Miss Thorne's Dancing Academy.

The little girl showed remarkable aptitude for the dance. When she was 10, she made her professional debut in a Christmas pantomime and convinced her family that there was more to her dancing than just exercise for health purposes. She was sent out to study under the severe tutelage of a famous Russian balletmaster. And Lillian Alicia Marks, as she grew sturdy and healthy, became Alicia Markova, one of the world's great ballerinas.

When she was 14, the remarkable little dancer caught the eye of the famous impresario, Serge Diaghileff. He was enchanted by the ethereal grace and fairy lightness of Alicia, who reminded him of the incomparable Pavlova. He engaged her to dance in his celebrated company in Monte Carlo.

A few years later, Alicia founded the Markova-Dolin Ballet, first English ballet company. With Anton Dolin as partner, she created and danced ballets all over England. With the passing of time, all the world saw her and gave her deserved acclaim as the first great English-born ballerina.

With the famous Sadler's Wells Ballet, Alicia created many roles. Among the best-known of these is "Giselle" and her dancing of this classic role is considered by critics to be the finest of modern times.

Alicia Markova, though an international star of the first magnitude, remained essentially the same simple, human and unspoiled person she was when she set out on her career. Having created many roles and proven herself one of the most versatile of performers, the prima ballerina of England is considered a model for all dancers, and one who belongs not only to Britain but to all the world.

Dr. LISE MEITNER

Hostess Of The Atomic Age

Many men labored on the once fantastic dream to bring civilization into the atomic age. But among all those famous pioneering men of science, stands one woman—as eminent a scientist, and important a physicist as the world ever has known. She is Doctor Lise Meitner. It was her research in atomic physics and her experiments in uranium fission that played a most vital part in the development of the greatest scientific achievement of this or any century.

She was born in Vienna, in 1878, the daughter of a lawyer. At an early age, Lise Meitner began to show a surprising interest in science. She began her science studies in Vienna where she became most interested in atomic physics.

In her early 20's she became tremendously inspired by the newspaper accounts of Marie Curie's great discovery of radium. She dreamed of emulating that famous Frenchwoman in scientific achievement.

In 1908, Lise Meitner came to Germany for advanced study in scientific research. By 1917, her fame as a scientist had become so eminent that she was entrusted with the organization of a department of physical radio activity at Berlin's famed Kaiser Wilhelm Institute. As professor and leading member of the Institute, Dr. Meitner won wide recognition for her research on the study of the natural and artificial transmutation of the elements, and her research on the products of the disintegration of radium, thorium and actinium, the behavior of the beta rays and on the physics of the atomic nucleus.

In 1933, when the Nazis began to take over the country, Lise Meitner was forced to flee from Germany to save her life. By the time the brilliant Dr. Meitner came to find refuge and a home in Sweden, she had solved the supposed barium mystery which had puzzled the greatest atomic scientists in the world. She made known her findings in a simple report for a scientific journal. It created a world sensation! For no scientist had split the atom into halves until she had proved that it could be done.

The results of her experiments were transmitted to Dr. Niel Bohr in the United States where the production of the atom bomb was a vast and secret project of the war department. It helped produce the first atom bomb in history!

Thrust into the universal spotlight as the most famous woman scientist in the world, Lise Meitner was reluctant to discuss her part in the development of the first atom bomb. Although, great was the clamor to see and hear this remarkable woman who was one of the architects of the atomic age, she shyly remained living quietly in Sweden. In 1945, she was elected a member of the Swedish Academy of Science, to share an honor that had been conferred on only one other woman scientist in history—the immortal Madame Marie Curie.

At 78, Dr. Lise Meitner was still busy with her scientific experiments, and her lectures at universities. Her fame in history is forever sure as that remarkable woman who helped make possible the atomic age.

Yehudi
MENUHIN

The Prodigy Who Grew Up Into A Genius

As a great master of the violin, Yehudi Menuhin is the first American-bred and trained virtuoso. The son of immigrants from Palestine, Yehudi showed at the fantastically early age of 2 that he was destined to follow a career in music. Unable to find a sitter to watch over him while his parents were at a concert, little Yehudi was taken along and amazed everyone around him by listening quietly and with complete absorption to the music. He was never thereafter left behind when his father and mother attended a concert.

One evening, his father brought him a little toy violin of tin. Yehudi first became angry, then cried, when he could not get any music out of it. So the little fellow was given a real violin, miniature in size, on which to play.

Almost instantly, it became clear that this was no ordinary child. Simple melodies came to him easily without any teaching. At 3, he began to take lessons. A year later, he was playing difficult classical compositions. And at 5, he made his first public appearance at a children's concert.

The child prodigy was soon playing with astonishing ability. The surprised critics spread the word, and offers poured in for the musical marvel to appear before audiences. But his father declined all of them because he considered the child too young. He was kept at home for the next four years, where his parents taught him not only the art of the violin but also literature and languages.

By the time he was 10, Yehudi had given only a few concerts, but his fame was already widespread. In the next year, he went on his first concert tour. His debuts in New York and Paris were sensational. When he was 12, an admirer presented him with a magnificent Stradivarius violin worth $60,000.

During the next few years, Yehudi Menuhin appeared everywhere to excited audiences. At 17, the whole world was at his feet. There was nothing in all violin literature that the youthful prodigy could not play perfectly. And when he came of age, at 21, he was a master violinist, one who could take his rightful place as a giant of music, the most renowned American violinist in the world.

Albert
Abraham
MICHELSON

First American for a Nobel Prize

American science has been enriched, in recent years, by the efforts and accomplishments of many Jewish mathematicians and physicists. Such outstanding names as Einstein, Fermi, Teller and Oppenheimer attest to their number and their prominence in the world of science. And yet, unique among them all, Albert Abraham Michelson stands out with special distinction. For it was he who, in 1907, was the first American scientist to win the coveted Nobel Prize.

Born in 1852 in Strelso near Poland, young Michelson was brought as a child to California by his father. When he finished his secondary schooling, the young man traveled alone from California to Washington, D.C. in order to make a personal plea to President U.S. Grant for an appointment to the United States Naval Academy. The President was so impressed by the determination of the young Jewish student that the plea was granted and young Michelson entered Annapolis.

At the Naval Academy, Michelson was a good if not remarkable student. However, he was outstanding in physics, and on his graduation, he was appointed an instructor at the Academy in that subject. His special study was the problem of light. To make his research more effective, he began to invent a series of remarkable instruments, best known of which was the interferometer by which it became possible to measure the tiniest quantity of space or matter with almost absolute exactitude.

Eventually Michelson, through his discoveries and inventions, was able to achieve one of the greatest scientific discoveries of the age when he computed the exact speed of light. This discovery helped pave the way for Einstein's theory of relativity, as well as making possible much of our present day knowledge of radioactivity, vitamins and hormones.

When Albert A. Michelson died in 1931, he had won fame and honors throughout the world. And while science today has more than its share of spectacular discoverers and inventors, his niche as America's first scientist to win the Nobel Prize is forever secure.

Henry
MORGENTHAU Jr.

Keeper Of A Nation's Purse

Although one other had held a post in the cabinet of a President before him, Henry Morgenthau, Jr., was the first Jew to become Secretary of the United States Treasury. He held that exalted and important post during twelve of the most turbulent years in American history.

Born in New York City in 1891, he was the son of a wealthy and distinguished father who had served the United States well, as Ambassador to Turkey. Young Morgenthau lived an uneventful life as a youth. He went to the proper private schools until he was 16, when he became bored with schooling, and became a drifter, to live an aimless life of a rich man's son.

In 1909, he entered Cornell University to study architecture, but he soon lost interest in that, too, and he left school to wander from job to job to no purpose. He drifted to Texas, and there he became interested in farming. He returned to school to study agriculture. To encourage what seemed to be a valid ambition, his rich father bought for him 1,400 acres of fertile farming land on the Hudson River. There, Henry Morgenthau, Jr., started growing apples for a livelihood.

Surprisingly enough, he made a great success of his farming venture. What was more significant, as a farmer, he became friends with a young man on a nearby estate, by the name of Franklin Delano Roosevelt. Their close friendship eventually led to a political association. In World War I when Morgenthau was rejected from Army service because of faulty eyesight, he went to work under Roosevelt when the latter was Assistant Secretary of the United States Navy. Later, when Roosevelt ran for Governor of New York, Morgenthau was his campaign manager. And in 1934, when F.D.R. became the President of the United States, Morgenthau, then only 42, went to Washington to serve his country as the Secretary of the Treasury. He was one of the youngest in American history.

He held that delicate post from 1934 to 1945, and in his high position, Morgenthau was responsible for the major task of financing World War II. He set up the United States War Savings Bond campaign. He ran the office of Secretary of the Treasury with exemplary efficiency.

After the war, Morgenthau became the first General Chairman of the United Jewish Appeal, and head of the American Financial and Development Corporation for Israel. Many important honors came to him as a public servant. But his place in history is assured as the first Jew to hold the second highest post in the cabinet of a President of the United States.

MOSES

A Prophet For All Eternity

When the people of Israel were living in bondage in Egypt, they began to grow great in number and strength. The new Pharaoh, fearful for his power, decreed that the new-born sons of the Hebrews be slaughtered at birth. Many were the ruses used by the Hebrew women to save their offspring. And one of them, when her son was born, placed him in a small cradle and set him afloat on the Nile near where the daughter of the Pharaoh was bathing with her friends.

Pharaoh's daughter saved the infant and brought him to the palace where she reared him as her own son. She named the child Moses, and his life was that of a prince. One day, when a young man, Moses saw an Egyptian overseer beating a Hebrew slave to death. He killed the Egyptian, and when word of what he had done reached Pharaoh, Moses fled for his life. He settled in the desert at Midian, married and raised a family. Then, at the command of God, he returned to Egypt to free his people and lead them to the land of milk and honey.

Moses and his people wandered in the desert for 40 years after escaping from Egypt.

It was with great difficulty that Moses managed to hold his people on the hard road to the goal promised by the Lord. On the way, Moses went atop Mount Sinai and brought down on stone tablets the Ten Commandments, the basic moral law not only for the Jews but for all the civilized world. Many were the laws and moral precepts that Moses laid down for his people. They are to be found in the Five Books of Moses, known also as the Pentateuch and Torah, containing the code of laws followed by the Jewish people from that day to this.

The time came at last when Moses reached the land of Canaan, flowing with milk and honey. From the top of Mount Pisgah, Moses looked down at the land the Lord had promised to his people. But he was not permitted to enter this Promised Land, only to see it. He died on the mountain at the age of 120 years, "his eye not dim, nor his natural force abated." No man knows the place of his burial, if buried he was. Legend has it that Moses disappeared on the mountain. He had given the Jews the Law by which they were to live. "And there has not arisen a prophet since in Israel like Moses, whom the Lord knew face to face."

Paul
MUNI

Elder Statesman Of The American Theatre

Reared in the fascinating insecurity of a theatre trunk, Paul Muni was from birth a child of the stage. His parents, strolling players of the European ghettos, took the child with them wherever they went. In their nomadic wanderings, the family eventually reached London where the boy, then Muni Weisenfreund, saw the inside of a school for the first time. In 1902, they came to America.

Schooling was haphazard for Muni, for the Weisenfreunds were still troupers in the Yiddish variety theatres, and they still took Muni along always. In the hope that he might become a musician, he began, at his father's insistence, to take violin lessons. But the pull of the stage was too strong. When other actors in the troupe fell ill, Muni filled in. At 13, he began his fantastic habit of playing very old bearded men. And when he became a regular member of the company, his father solemnly broke his son's violin across his knee. Destiny had made its choice.

For the next 18 years, Muni played everything in Yiddish from Ibsen to burlesque. Always he showed his remarkable flair in the use of make-up. In 1918, Maurice Schwartz, an-

other famous actor and producer, spotted Muni and brought him into his Yiddish Art Theatre.

In 1926, the 31-year-old Muni Weisenfreund took the new name of Paul Muni and moved over to the American stage. He was an instantaneous hit. He never returned to the Yiddish stage. Eventually Hollywood called him, and Paul Muni made some of the greatest films ever produced there, like "Scarface," the best of its type, "Pasteur," "Zola," "Juarez," and many others. Honors were many, including the Academy Award.

In 1955, at 60, Paul Muni, now an elder statesman of the American theatre, was starring in a new play in a role for which he had received the highest praise of his life. After a few weeks, he fell ill. He entered a hospital where he learned that one of his eyes had to be removed. The shock to Paul Muni was as nothing compared to that which struck deep into the hearts of theatregoers everywhere. The world bade a sad farewell to Paul Muni, the actor.

A few weeks later, Paul Muni, celebrated character actor, stepped back into his role on Broadway, minus an eye, but as great a performer as ever. For he would not stop acting as long as he could walk out upon a stage.

[88]

GOLDA MYERSON

From School Marm To Israeli Foreign Minister

She was born Golda Madovitz, in Kiev, Russia, in 1898. When she was eight years old, her family emigrated to the United States, and her father settled in Milwaukee to work as a humble and obscure carpenter.

Golda's girlhood was without distinction. She attended public schools and a teacher's college without attracting any notice either as a brilliant scholar or a popular girl. Plain-looking in appearance, gentle in manner, and serious in purpose, she became a schoolteacher. A drab and unexciting life devoid of any fame or drama seemed to be her future. But at 23, she married an ardent Zionist, and as Mrs. Golda Myerson she suddenly found herself plunged into a new, exciting and most adventurous life beyond her wildest expectations.

With her husband, she went to Palestine where she became a chicken farmer on a collective farm. She drifted into trade union work, and by 1928, she had become so well known that she was elected a director of the Women's Labor Council. In time, she became secretary-general of the Palestine General Federation of Jewish Labor. Mrs. Golda Myerson also became a hard-working, forceful pioneer in Israel's struggle for independence—one of the most dramatic personalities in the history of Zionism. Often she gambled with her freedom and at times even with her life to help win independence for the land she loved.

In 1948, Mrs. Golda Myerson became the first Israeli ambassador to Russia. While there, she staged not only many sharp and dramatic public verbal clashes with the leaders of the Soviet Union, for the cause of Zionism, but she also inspired many wild demonstrations by thousands of Russian Jews who always swarmed to the streets of Moscow to see and greet the widely known and loved Goldie Myerson on her way to the synagogue for Holy Day services.

She returned to Israel to become minister of labor and social welfare. In that post, she earned an awesome reputation. Prime Minister Ben Gurion often said of her: "In the Cabinet, Goldie is the only real man!"

At 58, Mrs. Golda Myerson had packed away a full and busy life for one woman—as a schoolteacher, wife, mother, chicken farmer, union organizer, political leader, diplomat, parliamentarian, business director, Cabinet officer, lecturer, and one of the leading figures in the political affairs of the Middle East. But in 1956, Golda Myerson achieved a new fame and a unique honor never before known by a Jewess, nor by any woman in world history. For she became Israel's foreign minister—the world's first woman foreign minister!

Ernesto NATHAN

A Mayor of Rome

In many of the famed cities of the world many Jews have achieved the honor and the prominence of the office of Mayor. But no Jew ever became the head of a large city under more bizarre circumstances than Ernesto Nathan. He was the most unique Mayor in history.

Who, one might ask, would be the least likely person to become the Mayor of a city like Catholic Rome? The answer would assuredly be a Jew who was a liberal, a militant Freemason, and an alien. And yet, precisely in Rome, the Eternal City of the Catholic faith, such a man did achieve the position of Mayor. Although, Ernesto Nathan pronounced his republicanism and anti-clericalism in the city of the Pope and the Vatican, the people of Rome elected him Mayor, again and again, by acclamation.

He was born in London, England, in 1845. As a boy, he met the Italian patriot, Giuseppe Mazzini, who was in exile from his native land. The spiritual leader of the Italian revolution was a frequent visitor to the home of Nathan's parents, and young Ernesto was strongly influenced by him.

When he was 14, his mother Sara Nathan took him for his first visit to Italy. Ernesto fell in love with that sunny land. When he grew older, he went to live in Rome, and he became the manager of the Roman newspaper "Roma del Popolo" founded by the patriot Mazzini. Brilliant and active in the life of Rome, when only 26, his home became the meeting place for Italy's most famous authors, celebrated scientists and important politicians.

At 44, Ernesto Nathan became an Italian citizen. In 1907, he created a world sensation when he was elected the Mayor of Rome. For only 40 years before, the Jewish ghetto had been demolished in that city. Ernesto Nathan achieved such popularity as Mayor of Rome that he was elected to term after term, by acclamation.

For six years he served as the Mayor of Rome, and upon his retirement from that post, he was further honored by being appointed a member of the Italian Senate. He served with distinction the nation and the people he had come to love with complete devotion. Even when he was 70 years of age, at the outbreak of the First World War, he insisted on enlisting in the Italian Army for active service. And as a first lieutenant, he saw action at the front.

He died in 1921. All Rome wept at the passing of Ernesto Nathan, the Jew, who had been the most distinguished and the most popular Mayor, Catholic Rome ever had.

Mordecai
Manuel
NOAH

The First Zionist

Mordecai Noah was one of the most colorful characters in the early history of the United States. The son of ardent patriots, Noah was born in Philadelphia in 1785. His earliest interest was the theatre. He wrote several successful plays. At 24, he became the editor of a newspaper. Four years later, when President Madison appointed him consul at Tunis in the Barbary States, he became the first Jew in America to hold a high diplomatic post in the foreign service. As consul, he succeeded in obtaining the release of a number of American sailors who had been captured by the pirates of North Africa and sold into slavery.

On his return to the United States, Noah founded and edited a number of newspapers, and became more and more involved in New York's public affairs. He served as High Sheriff of the city, and Surveyor of the Port and Judge of the Court of General Sessions.

As a newspaper owner and editor, Noah founded a pioneer newsgathering agency and did much to raise the general level of journalism in the United States. As a playwright, he continued all through life to write successful dramas for the theatre.

But it is not for these alone that Noah deserves to be remembered. In 1825, Mordecai Noah embarked on one of the most unusual and spectacular affairs in Jewish history. Giving himself the title of "Governor and Judge of Israel," Noah proclaimed the re-establishment of the government of the Jewish nation under the auspices and protection of the Constitution and the laws of the United States. He purchased a tract of 17,000 acres on Grand Island in the Niagara River near Buffalo, as a site for a Jewish settlement. He named it Ararat, the City of Refuge for the Jews. He issued a manifesto to Jews all over the world, inviting them to come and settle in Ararat.

The scheme was quixotic and doomed to failure. Although the idea stirred Jews in all parts of the civilized world, none appeared at the dedication ceremonies save Noah himself. But the whole affair did give Noah a permanent niche in Jewish history as the first political Zionist, a man who sought to establish a homeland for Jews many decades before Herzl.

Jacques OFFENBACH

The Tales Of Hoffman

As the son of a synagogue cantor in Cologne, Jacques Offenbach showed at an early age that he was musically gifted. At 6, he was a highly skillful violinist. At the same time, he yearned to play the cello, but his father feared that the instrument was too unwieldy for his frail little son and Jacques had to practice in secret. Then, one day, he startled his family by filling in at a concert when the regular cellist failed to show up. From then on, he played the cello regularly in the family trio. And he wrote little songs.

The elder Offenbach soon realized that his son was destined to be more than just another instrumentalist. He took the boy to Paris and entered him in the conservatory where the youngster impressed the authorities with the quality of his playing. Offenbach studied for a year and then left to join the orchestra of the Opéra Comique. And in his free time, he began to compose.

Offenbach's compositions failed to impress anybody for a long time. He became the musical director of the Comédie Française in 1850 and held that post for five years. Then, since no one wanted to produce his work, he left the Comédie and opened his own theatre. There his opera bouffe or burlesque opera was immediately successful. It was a new type of music and the Paris audiences were enchanted by it. He became the darling of the boulevards and his music was played and sung everywhere. The French government rewarded him by bestowing on him the ribbon of the Legion of Honor.

But times grew bad for Offenbach after a while, and his fame and fortune waned. He went to America where he scored new successes. In England, too, he was well-received. But his heart belonged in Paris. He returned there a sick and wasted man and began to work against time on his most important and most serious work that would be his musical legacy to the world. When he finished the opera, which he called "The Tales of Hoffman," he pleaded for a quick production since he felt that he had so little time to live. However, luck was not with him. Offenbach never heard the first performance of his great and immortal opera. He died on October 4, 1880, without knowing that he had produced one of the greatest and most popular operatic scores in musical history. "The Tales of Hoffman" remains with grateful music lovers as a glowing monument to his greatness.

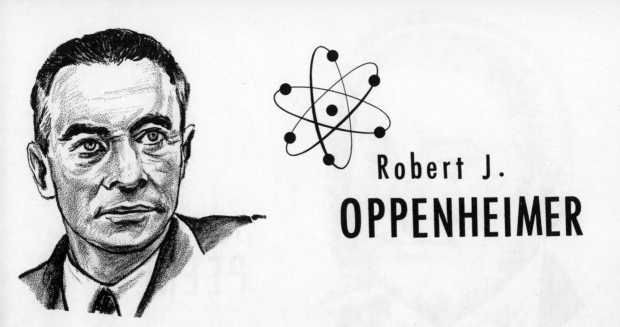

Robert J. OPPENHEIMER

He Unlocked The Door To The Atomic Age

Born in New York in 1904, he was the son of a German immigrant who became a prosperous textile manufacturer. Painfully shy and timid, he developed into a quiet and studious boy. At 12, he was already a better than average mineralogist. By the time he was ready to enter Harvard University, he had a full and intimate knowledge of Greek and Latin, wrote sonnets in French, and was engrossed in mathematics and the sciences. He graduated from Harvard in 3 years, "summa cum laude" and went to study at Cambridge in England and Gottingen, Germany, where he took his Ph.D. at 23.

Having developed into a master physicist, Oppenheimer returned to America to become a professor at the University of California, in 1929. For 10 years, there poured from his classroom a steady stream of brilliant physicists. Because of him as a college professor, the United States is now enriched with many top physicists whose principal goal is to imitate the brilliance of Oppenheimer, their teacher.

Then World War II broke out. Though he was purely a teacher and theoretician, the United States turned to this shy professor to direct and boss the production of the first atom bomb in history. It was a secret sixty-million dollar project. The world's leading scientists, even those who disliked him personally, flocked to Oppenheimer and the great project the government set up in the desert of New Mexico.

For over two years, Oppenheimer struggled with the great task to produce the first atom bomb, as he supervised, guided and directed the greatest collection of scientific minds ever assembled in one place. His hair turned gray, his weight fell to 120 pounds, as he gave all his energy to complete the greatest experiment of the 20th century. And under him, the project achieved success, and the world's first atom bomb was produced. It won World War II.

After the success of the great Los Alamos project, Oppenheimer turned to more peaceful pursuits. He became the director of the world-famed Institute for Advanced Studies at Princeton, New Jersey, where the genius of mathematics, Einstein, studied and worked until his death. There, Oppenheimer gathered many of the finest young physicists from all over the world to teach them theoretical physics.

A complex man, few have understood him. Noted for the clarity and beauty of his speech and writings, he has given his life to seeking and speaking the truth. And always history will accord him his true place for fame—the man who unlocked the Atomic Door for the 20th century.

Jan
PEERCE

Golden Voice Of The Met

When Jacob Pincus Perelmuth was a boy on New York's East Side, his father induced him to take violin lessons in order to acquire a little culture. But the boy had a naturally good voice, and he sang continually, either in the synagogue with the choir on the High Holy Days, or with the little orchestra he put together for neighborhood dances. When he was 15, he found a job in a Catskill Mountain resort and there, for the next 14 summers, he played his fiddle and sang vocal refrains.

As the years passed, the boy continued to prepare himself for bigger and better things. He dreamed of a career on the Broadway stage. When Roxy, the famous impresario of Radio City Music Hall, heard him sing, he signed him for a four-week trial at that famous theatre. He also induced Jacob Pincus Perelmuth to change his name to one that would look better in lights. The young man took the name of Jan Peerce.

Jan Peerce worked hard for his debut. But when the time came for him to sing at the Music Hall the show ran too long and his song was left out. Then Roxy fell ill and Jan Peerce

was entirely forgotten. At last, a chance came for him to sing—but from the wings and not on stage. No one saw him—but everyone heard him and his glorious voice stopped the show.

Jan Peerce was hired on the spot to be the permanent singer at the world-famed Radio City Music Hall. He remained there for 5 years, and was its biggest attraction during that time. Meanwhile, he continued to study and learn. In 1938, he had an audition with Toscanini, the famous conductor. When Jan Peerce finished singing, the great Italian maestro exclaimed, "Che bella voce!" and promptly hired him to sing as soloist with his symphony orchestra.

Now all doors opened to Jan Peerce. He went from triumph to triumph, and in 1941, he became the leading tenor at the famed Metropolitan Opera House, and in 1956, he was still there. As a guest artist, he also sang with every famous opera company and symphony orchestra in the world.

The one-time synagogue choir boy and popular ballad singer of the music halls turned out to be America's foremost opera tenor, the greatest since the golden days of the immortal Enrico Caruso.

Joseph
PULITZER

He Shook A Nation With His Newspaper

To Joseph Pulitzer fell the unique honor of being the first Jew in America to have his picture on a United States postage stamp. The father of the flaming headline was so remembered in 1947, on the 100th anniversary of the date of his birth.

Born in Hungary, Joseph Pulitzer came to America when he was 17. The year was 1864, and young Pulitzer, who had been rejected by the Hungarian army because of an eye defect, enlisted in the Union Army to fight in the Civil War. After being demobilized, the young Hungarian, penniless and homeless, made his way west. He studied law and was admitted to the bar at 21. But he found the practice of law too tame. A dynamo of mental and physical energy, Pulitzer grabbed the chance to become a reporter on a St. Louis newspaper. He rose to be managing editor, then part owner. In 1869, he was elected to the Missouri legislature. And in 1878—when he was 31—he took over a dying newspaper and combined it with another to form the *St. Louis Post-Dispatch*. Five years later, his dynamic leadership and courageous truth-telling made the new paper one of America's greatest successes, bringing him an income of $150,000 a year.

Although his health was poor and doctors warned him to cut down on his activities, Pulitzer bought the *New York World,* an unimpressive and unsuccessful newspaper. He built it up to be the most popular and most profitable one in the United States.

Pulitzer's success was due to many factors. He fought corruption and demagogues in all parties. He advocated reform and progress in the interest of the common people. He was completely fearless in his attacks on wrong and oppression.

Pulitzer became a chronic invalid and blind, but he never let up in his activities to the day he died. He made millions of dollars, but his benefactions have made his name a byword in the world of journalism and literature. He gave Columbia University $2,000,000 to found a school of journalism and he set up the Pulitzer Scholarship Fund for journalism students to study abroad. His most famous award, however, is the Pulitzer Prize, given annually to the best American play and novel and to various "bests" in the field of journalism.

Samuel
RESHEVSKY

Grand Master Of Chess

There are many fields of activity in which Jews have been particularly adept. In none have they been more so than in the ancient and absorbing game of chess. Among the great Jewish players, no chess master has so fascinating a story as Samuel Reshevsky who, at 43, had been for 39 years one of the world's greatest exponents of the most intellectual sport of all.

Descendant of a rabbinical family, Samuel Reshevsky was born in a little Polish village near Lodz. Before he had reached his fourth birthday, little Samuel was already watching his father, a pious and orthodox Jew, playing chess with his cronies. After a couple of months of close observation, the little boy startled his father by challenging him to a game. Amused and pleased, the elder Reshevsky set up the pieces. After a few quick moves, the game was over. Little Sammy had won.

Sammy's father immediately spread the news around the village. A new chess prodigy had appeared! The boy was rushed off to the Lodz Chess Club to demonstrate his prowess. He played 12 simultaneous games and won them all. A year or so later, he toured Poland, giving remarkable demonstrations of his skill. By the time he was 8, he had toured all Europe under his father's management, and startled chess masters everywhere with his phenomenal mastery of the ancient game. And his earnings from his exhibitions fortunately supplied a much-needed income for his family.

In 1920, Samuel Reshevsky, aged 9, came to America. The *wunderkind* of chess made as deep an impression in the United States as he had in Europe. He appeared in many simultaneous exhibition matches without ever being defeated. For years, he was the greatest player in the land, and in 1935 he became an international Grand Master, defeating, among others, the redoubtable world champion, Jose Capablanca. In all his years of play, Reshevsky has never lost a man-to-man contest nor finished lower than third in any tournament. He won the United States championship four times in a row, and five times in all.

Reshevsky has been, at all times, devoted to orthodox Jewry, never playing on the Sabbath and even sacrificing a European championship once to return to America for the High Holy Days. Outstanding as a child prodigy, he grew up to even greater fame and prestige as a grand master of chess.

Admiral Hyman RICKOVER

Man Behind The Atomic Sub

There is no more graphic proof of the peculiar affinity of Jews to science than the subject of atomic energy. First, it was the Jew, Einstein, who gave us the theory. Then it was the Jew, Oppenheimer, who first applied the theory to the making of that massive destroyer, the atomic bomb. And it was again a Jew, Hyman Rickover, who turned atomic energy to non-destructive purposes with the world's first atom-driven submarine.

Hyman Rickover, who was born in Russia in 1900, was the son of a Chicago tailor. Having attended public schools, young Rickover was appointed to the Naval Academy and commissioned an ensign in 1922. After a tour of duty at sea, he returned to Annapolis and then Columbia University to continue his studies in electrical engineering.

It was in 1946, after a career of submarine duty and surface-vessel command, that the idea of an atomic-power-driven submarine first occurred to him. He worked out a plan for such a submarine and submitted it to the Navy. The plan was shelved but Rickover appealed to Admiral Nimitz, Chief of Naval Operations, who went to bat for him. When Congress, at last, voted a large sum of money for the dream project in 1951, work began on the ship no one could describe and only a handful of men believed could be built.

The fantastic obstacles that Rickover had to overcome, the struggle he fought to get the necessary personnel to work with him, the sheer newness of the whole idea, are now a matter of history. In 1952, Rickover's dream, the first atomic submarine called the "Nautilus" was launched. The deadliest weapon of the sea ever devised was a reality!

Captain Rickover received medals and commendations from all sides but he was on the verge of being retired from the Navy in 1952, having been passed over for promotion twice under the Navy's antiquated rules. The "Nautilus" was then not yet ready, and may never have been completed had such a tragedy been allowed to take place. But President Eisenhower himself intervened personally. In 1956, the creator of the atomic submarine wore the stripes of a rear admiral and was busily engaged on bigger and better atomic-powered submarines yet to be built.

Elias A. **RIES**

The Forgotten Inventor

Great inventors usually reap either fortunes from their work or fame. But Elias E. Ries, one of the world's greatest inventors, producer of more than 250 important patents which earned millions for others and made possible some of the world's most important industrial enterprises, ended his days not only a poor man but also a completely forgotten one.

Born in Germany in 1862, Ries was brought to America by his deeply religious parents to escape persecution. As a child, he loved to tinker, but when 13 he was obliged to leave school to earn his keep. He worked in his father's shoe store in Baltimore, but spent most of his time around the machinery in the shop. Other than a little mechanical drawing, he received no further training. Nevertheless, he mastered, all by himself, the intricacies of electrical science.

At 19, he began his experiments. He developed and obtained a patent for a railroad crossing light alarm. He patented a process for electrical welding, and a process to harden and temper steel. Many things he worked out he was too poor to patent. In 1888, one of his inventions was at last put to general use. It was the electric elevator safety control, an invention that made the skyscraper possible.

He was still poor and unknown when, in 1896, he succeeded in synchronizing motion and sound on a single film. He invented the crown bottle cap. A tube welding patent brought him $1,000, and it was 30 years before it came into common use and earned millions for others. Westinghouse bought 65 of his patents for less than $1,000 each and went on to become an industrial giant. His sound-on-film invention, basic to sound films, came so early that no producer dared to put it to use. In 1925, his patent, obtained in 1896, was bought for a mere $3,000!

Nor did he do less for his country. During World War I, Ries invented an instrument for detecting submarines by an echo system. This device was instrumental in winning World War II!

When Ries died in 1928, an undeserved curtain of silence fell on the brilliant, unknown career of one of the world's greatest inventors whose main fault was that he came before his time.

ERNESTINE L. ROSE

First Woman Reformer

Although she was born in the obscurity of Pyeterkow, Poland, the daughter of a pious and humble rabbi, she became one of the most fascinating and important women in American history.

She came into the world in 1810, as Sismondi Potowski. Something of an infant prodigy, at an early age she was taught Hebrew, Jewish lore, and the strict observance of all the rites and ceremonies of the Jewish faith. But when she was only 14, she shocked the orthodox community of her native village by refusing to accept the literal interpretation of the Bible as it was taught. Moreover, she boldly advocated equal rights for women in all spheres of community life.

When Sismondi Potowski was 16 years old, upon her mother's death, she left home to see the great world. Alone, she visited Poland, Russia, Holland, Belgium, Germany, France and England. Wherever she went, she was a fearless and outspoken advocate of equal rights for women in a man's world.

At 26, she married an Englishman named William Rose, and in 1836, she came to America. Soon, the new growing country began to hear much of Ernestine Rose as a militant reformer. This Polish-Jewess became a zealous pioneer in the movement to gain freedom, justice and equality for American women. And, while vigorously fighting for Woman's Rights and woman suffrage, she also found time to challenge all the other evils of her day—Negro slavery, religious bigotry, unspeakable living conditions of the working masses, neglect of the poor and the weak, excessive drinking, and all the other social maladjustments then plaguing a growing America.

Because she was an alien and a Jewess, she met with bitter and violent antagonism when she dared challenge the evils of her day, but so eloquent was her voice, so impressive was her womanly poise and dignity on a public platform, so great her tact, and so vibrant her personality and charm, that she became the most popular public lecturer of her time, and a world-wide celebrity. So she remained for a quarter of a century.

Ernestine Rose gave herself so selflessly to the great cause of full emancipation of the American woman that she wrecked her health. In 1869, sick and weary, she was forced to retire from all public activity. She returned to England to live there as an invalid, until she died in 1892.

Forgotten she may be now as the first, most militant and most celebrated Jewish woman reformer, but her place in history is secure as a vibrant part of the soul of the women's rights movement in America. No Jewess fought more valiantly nor pioneered more potently in the cause that eventually won the freedom, the prestige, the influence, the respect, the social, political and economical independence which American womanhood now accepts as commonplace.

[99]

Anna
ROSENBERG

Little Woman Of Giant Stature

Never has there been, among Jewish women, a more unusual or more extraordinary career than that of tiny Anna Rosenberg. For this dynamic and brilliant bundle of energy has held not only the highest post ever filled by a woman in the American military establishment but was the first Jewish woman in United States history to hold any high federal post.

A wife at 18 and a mother at 20, the little girl who had left Budapest, Hungary, at 10, found herself running a successful business as a labor consultant when she was only 23. Her talent for such work had developed early, for she had helped mediate a students' strike during World War I and headed delegations to city officials on behalf of her fellow high school students.

By the late 1920's, Anna Rosenberg was reputedly the busiest woman in New York, so successful in her work as a labor consultant and public relations counsel, that her income was over $60,000 a year. Not only were her services sought by the largest business firms in the country, but city and state officials consulted her about their problems. As time passed, she took

on more and more work for government bodies. In 1938, President Roosevelt sent her abroad to study industrial relations for him. In 1944, he sent her to Europe as his personal observer and a year later, she went again to help President Truman untangle the great problems of repatriation and demobilization of our troops there.

Meanwhile, she had served as the only woman regional director of the War Manpower Commission. And her services to the United States was finally capped in 1950 when Secretary of Defense George C. Marshall appointed her Assistant Secretary. Although she was bitterly attacked as a woman—a Jewish woman to boot—the Senate overwhelmingly approved the appointment. In her new post, she became the adviser of generals and the boss of millions of soldiers.

For her great services, Anna Rosenberg was awarded the Medal of Merit, first woman in history to be so honored. There were many other honors that came the way of the dynamic little Mrs. Rosenberg whose contributions to her country had been unique and who held posts no one ever dreamed could come to a Jewish woman.

Yossele ROSENBLATT

The Little Cantor

Many years have passed since the death of the celebrated cantor, Yossele Rosenblatt, but even today, almost every Jewish home that holds a phonograph possesses at least one cherished record of his great voice.

Born in a Ukrainian ghetto village in 1882, Yossele Rosenblatt was the first son in a family already blessed with nine daughters. He was very small as a boy, nor did he ever grow to normal height. Everyone called him "little Yossele" and listened to his golden voice with wonder.

When he was 5, Yossele began to assist his father, an obscure small-town cantor, as a regular member of the synagogue choir. His beautiful voice excited so much comment that he soon began to tour neighboring towns where strangers could hear the cantor prodigy.

His father took him farther and farther from home, and the boy began to earn as much as $4 an appearance, a fortune for the Rosenblatt family. Long before his bar mitzvah, Yossele was a celebrated cantor. At 14, he was hailed in Vienna as the world's youngest cantor. Wherever he performed throughout Europe, he met with great acclaim.

In 1909, the American delegates to a World Zionist Congress in Hamburg heard the young cantor sing. They were so deeply impressed that an offer was made to him to come to America. There, an orthodox congregation in New York paid him $2,400 a year, the highest salary ever paid a cantor.

His success in America was fabulous. The Jews acclaimed him as the greatest cantor ever heard. Even people of other faiths came to the synagogue to hear his beautiful voice. He refused an offer of $1,000 a night to sing in opera because he considered it incompatible with his role as a cantor. Nevertheless, in response to great pressure, he agreed to make several concert tours of America and Europe so that all the world could hear his voice. And through the medium of phonograph records, countless millions of people thrilled to his golden voice singing the traditional music of the synagogue. The little cantor came to earn more than $75,000 a year!

After years of fabulous success as the "Singer of the Lord" in all parts of the world, he yearned to visit "Eretz Israel" and sing there for the Hebrew people. He went to Palestine, and the people went wild over him.

In Jerusalem, he sang for the last time in a synagogue. After conducting a Sabbath service, he suffered a heart attack and died. He was only 51. They buried Yossele Rosenblatt in the Mount of Olives Cemetery, the oldest and most sacred in the Holy Land, as all the Jews of the world wept for the loss of Jewry's greatest and most beloved cantor.

Julius
ROSENWALD

A Most Unusual Philanthropist

It is expected that a wealthy Jew will share his affluence with his less fortunate brethren. And yet, the benefactions of Julius Rosenwald hold a unique place in Jewish philanthropy. For it was not only to his own needy and oppressed that Rosenwald opened his heart, but to a people even poorer and less endowed, the American Negro in the South.

After working a while in his uncle's clothing store in New York, Julius Rosenwald opened a shop of his own in 1884 when he was 23. A year later he was bankrupt. He went to Chicago where he started a clothing factory. In nine years, he had worked himself up to a comfortable fortune and part-ownership of Sears, Roebuck, a mail order firm. He developed that company to its present enormous size and prominence through his policies of truth in advertising and a money-back guarantee.

Having made a great fortune, Rosenwald turned seriously to his philanthropies. He never asked what color or creed a contribution was asked for. He set up a staff of experts to advise him on his benefactions, to make sure they would do the most good.

He gave to hospitals, schools, organizations. He helped build the University of Chicago to a great institution, and financed the Museum of Science and Industry. But help to the Negro became his outstanding life work. He gave to build 26 YMCA and 3 YWCA buildings, as well as 50 other small buildings for the recreational use of the Negro in the South. With the help and approval of Booker T. Washington, eminent Negro educator and leader, he worked out a plan for building rural schools. These were erected by the hundreds until there were some 5,337 new Rosenwald schools in 15 Southern states, with 700,000 Negro children taught by 15,000 Negro teachers. Thousands of the children who suffered from pellagra were cured through blood tests paid for by Rosenwald and treated by doctors supplied free by him.

Today thousands of schools and homes in the South proudly hang the picture of Julius Rosenwald beside the pictures of their other heroes, Abraham Lincoln and Booker T. Washington.

Dr. Jonas SALK

Conqueror Of Polio

At the age of 40, Doctor Jonas E. Salk became world-famous as the discoverer of the anti-polio vaccine that bears his name. Today he is an immortal in medicine's hall of fame. But it was an odd set of circumstances that led the quiet, modest and friendly scientist to one of the world's most outstanding discoveries in the constant struggle against the dread diseases of mankind.

Born in 1914, Jonas Salk attended the public schools of New York. He was a very bright student, but there was nothing to indicate what the future held in store for him. The son of a small manufacturer, Salk played tennis and baseball like other boys, was affable and friendly and well-liked. He entered City College of New York at the early age of 15. His intention was to study law, but, as a freshman, he suddenly decided to add a science course to his curriculum, purely to give himself a broader background. At once he saw where his real interests lay. From then on, his life was to be all science. He entered New York University's School of Medicine. There, after his first year, he won a fellowship in chemistry, and again his career shifted emphasis. He went on to take his degree in medicine, but now his full interest was in research. He worked on the development of the flu vaccine and the National Research Council, in 1942, gave him another fellowship at the University of Michigan. There, he helped discover the commercial flu vaccines now on the market.

In 1947, Dr. Salk accepted the offer of the University of Pittsburgh to set up a special virus laboratory. And he began to work on his major task while continuing with research into flu vaccines. The search for a means to control polio was a historic one. For years, scientists had sought in vain a means to control that scourge which was crippling and killing children. Working with dogged determination, often 20 hours a day, Dr. Salk finally discovered the vaccine he thought would work. To prove it, it had to be tested on humans—and Dr. Salk chose to use himself and his own children as subjects for that experimental injection. When that worked, further experiments continued on a broader scale with many other children. And then, in 1955, on a red-letter day in medical history, the news burst on an anxiously waiting world. Another dreadful disease had been conquered.

Jonas Salk's anti-polio vaccine now has become man's most powerful weapon to beat back the forces of the disease of paralytic polio.

Long chapters will be printed in medical textbooks to reveal man's efforts to overcome virus diseases. None will be brighter than that dealing with Jonas Salk's victory over polio—to protect all the children of the world!

Haym
SOLOMON

Unknown Hero Of The American Revolution

When the War for Independence began in the American colonies in 1775, many brave and patriotic men joined the raw, new army to fight for freedom from British tyranny. Those men were heroes, and their struggle is truly an epic of courage and devotion to a cause.

But there were others who fought the good fight in their own way whose contributions to the ultimate victory cannot be slighted to any degree. Among them was a young banker in New York named Haym Salomon. The first Jew to come to these shores from Poland, Salomon had been a prosperous merchant in his native Lissa. He was an educated and sensitive man, a master of many languages.

When the Revolution came, Salomon, who had been here but 5 years, immediately ranged himself on the side of the colonies against Britain. A rich man who could have lived comfortably and in relative peace, Salomon poured out his wealth in aid of the American cause, and

when his own money gave out, sought financial help from others.

Even when he was arrested by the British and sentenced to death for helping the Revolution, Salomon continued to work for the Americans. He assisted patriotic prisoners to escape and created dissension among the Hessian officers, causing many of them to come over to the American side. And finally he escaped himself.

By the end of the war, Salomon had not only raised huge sums from others for guns and supplies for General George Washington, but he had impoverished himself by giving $650,-000 of his own funds to the new nation. He was able to recoup his fortune to some extent, but he continued to lend money to the struggling government. At last, impoverished anew and in failing health, Haym Salomon, silent soldier of the American Revolution, died in 1785, leaving his wife and children penniless. Neither he nor his heirs ever got back a penny of the huge sums he had advanced to the new United States government. He was buried in the old Jewish cemetery of the Mikveh Israel Congregation in the city of Philadelphia.

Francis
SALVADOR

The First Life For American Independence

To Francis Salvador belongs the unique distinction of being the first Jew to die in the American Revolution. Born an aristocrat, he had amassed wealth at an early age, only to be wiped out in the collapse of the Dutch East India Company. Determined to make a new start, Salvador came to the American colonies in 1773 and settled in South Carolina. In a short time, he had a plantation of some 7,000 acres, and was well on his way to recouping his lost fortune.

But there was a ferment in the colonies, and it soon took possession of Salvador too. A year after he landed in America, the new patriot was elected, first to the Provincial Congress, then to the General Assembly of South Carolina. Thus, he became the first Jew to hold public office in the American colonies. In his awakened fervor for republicanism, he became a close intimate of all the great revolutionary leaders.

In 1776, when the British troops landed at Charleston and, with the help of the Cherokee Indians, began to overrun the colony, Salvador took command of a body of militia and led a night attack against the enemy. In the battle, Salvador was wounded three times and then scalped by the Indians. Near death, he refused to be removed from the battlefield to a hospital. All he wanted was to know how the battle went. Assured by his men that victory was theirs, Francis Salvador died with a smile on his lips.

So, sadly, a life that was so full of promise for the future of the new country was snuffed out. He was barely 29 when his death came in his adopted country's struggle for freedom.

SAMSON

The World's Strongest Man

In ancient times, Samson was a judge among the Hebrews when the Philistines were their most powerful enemy in Palestine. While the Hebrews were weak, Samson himself was the strongest man in the world. Almost alone, he stood between the mighty forces of the Philistines and his panic-stricken people. Legends that have come down to us tell of the almost incredible strength of Samson. Once, he was attacked by a lion. With ease he tore it to pieces with his powerful hands. Again, when infuriated with the Philistines, he picked up the jawbone of an ass and with it smote the enemy, killing a thousand of them.

The Philistines feared and hated Samson but they did not know how to cope with him. The secret of his superhuman strength was hidden from them. Finally they bribed Delilah, a Philistine woman, to pry his secret from him. In time, he told her that his strength lay in his unshorn hair. That night, Delilah sent men to cut his hair as he slept. Then the weakened Samson was attacked and overcome, and taken to Gaza in chains.

In the great temple of the god, Dagon, Samson was placed on display for the Philistines to laugh at and mock. For weeks he had been laboring like an animal in a dark prison where he turned a treadmill to grind corn. Now, as he stood, blind and weak, between the pillars of the temple, Samson sent up a prayer. "Strengthen me, O Lord, only this once," he prayed, "that I may be avenged!"

Much time had passed since Samson had been captured and his eyes gouged out, and the hair on his head had grown long. Leaning on the pillars, he felt his prayer answered as his strength returned to his body. He grasped the pillars and leaned his weight upon them, saying, "Let me die with them."

Then Samson, the strongest man in history, pressed with all his might, and the great temple crumbled down on the heads of all the assembled lords of the Philistines. More died there than Samson had ever slain in all his life. And he died with them, as he had prayed. Nevertheless, Samson still lives as a symbol of superhuman strength. To tell a man that he is "as strong as Samson" is the highest praise even to this day.

SARAH

Mother Of The Hebrews

As Abraham is known to Jews as the father of Israel, so is Sarah, his wife, known as the great matriarch, mother of the Hebrew people. For it was from the son of Abraham and Sarah that all Jews are said to be descended.

The simple and moving details of the ancient Biblical story tell of Sarah who was a girl of great beauty and charm when she first married Abraham in Ur of the Chaldeans. The years passed but their marriage was not blessed with children and the unhappy Sarah became sharp of tongue and bitter of heart.

Then, in the land of Canaan, the Lord spoke to Abraham and promised him a son. Abraham laughed at the promise. "Shall a child be born to a man who is 100 years old?" he asked. "Shall Sarah, who is 90 years old, bear a child?"

Sarah, too, laughed bitterly at the promise of the Lord, but even as she did so she was afraid. For the Lord, hearing her laugh, said sternly, "Is anything too hard for the Lord? At the appointed time, Sarah shall have a son."

And so it came to pass that when the appointed time did come, Sarah bore a son to her husband, Abraham. The infant was named Isaac, and he was loved and cherished by his mother as no other child in history ever was. For his coming was nothing less than a miracle, and the Lord's promise that through this son she would be the mother of a great nation was for Sarah a promise of eternal life.

As the Bible says, Sarah lived "a hundred and twenty-seven years; these were the years of the life of Sarah." She died in Hebron in the land of Canaan, and the mourning Abraham put her to rest in the cave of Machpelah that he had bought especially for her burial. Abraham lived on for nearly 40 years more, and he lamented the loss of his faithful wife, Sarah, for the rest of his days.

David
SARNOFF

He Opened The World For Communication

As a child in Russia, David Sarnoff looked forward to some day becoming a rabbi. However, everything changed when he was brought to America at the age of 9. The year was 1900 and the Twentieth Century, symbolically speaking, came to America on the same boat. For it was under David Sarnoff's leadership that a whole new world of communication opened up, changing the face of the globe and altering beyond recognition the relations between men and history.

Left an orphan at 15, Sarnoff found a job as a messenger boy with the Marconi Wireless Telegraph Company. Radio fascinated him, and he spent many long hard hours learning what it was all about. He became a radio operator, both on land and on sea.

In 1912, Sarnoff was operator of the telegraph station in John Wanamaker's in New York. On the night of April 14th, he was the first to receive the wireless message from the ill-fated *Titanic* on its maiden voyage from England to New York. "We've struck an iceberg," the message read. "Sinking fast."

When Sarnoff flashed out the terrible news, orders came from Washington that all other radio operators were to leave the air. Only Sarnoff, for 17 gruelling hours, stayed in communication with the stricken ship. And it was he alone who obtained the pitifully short list of survivors before the great vessel finally sank to the bottom of the Atlantic. Only 706 were saved out of 2,223 aboard.

This devotion to duty was only the beginning of one of America's most fantastic careers in business. Sarnoff went on to become the first Jewish radio station manager in 1921. In 1926, he started the first great radio network—the National Broadcasting Company, and he became its president. Later, as head of the Radio Corporation of America, he rose to be one of the country's industrial giants, responsible for the universal use of radio and television, for the widest research in the field of communications, with more than 50,000 employees in one of America's most far-flung businesses. To his fame as an industrial leader, Sarnoff, during World War II, added distinction to his career by serving as brigadier-general on the staff of General Dwight Eisenhower.

As a radio and television pioneer, David Sarnoff is a man for many firsts. Because of him, the first political convention was broadcast and televised, as was the first major league baseball game, the first football game, and the first prizefight. He introduced radio's first classical music appreciation hour to an American audience, and he arranged for the first broadcast of an opera from the Metropolitan Opera House. Also, he was the first to bring the world-famed maestro Arturo Toscanini to radio to conduct a symphony orchestra.

SAUL

Israel's First King

When the people of Israel were sorely beset by the Philistines after the death of Samson had left them leaderless, they demanded of Samuel, the prophet and judge, that he give them a king to rule over them. Israel had never had a king. From the time of Moses they had been taught to believe that there was only One who could rule over them, and that was the Lord. But the people were insistent. Samuel sought the guidance of the Lord. He told the prophet to provide a king for Israel.

The choice to be first king of Israel fell on Saul, a simple farmer of the tribe of Benjamin. A brave fighter and an able commander of men, Saul proved every inch a king. Although a vengeful and moody man, he united the scattered tribes of Israel, organized and led armies against the enemies of his people and defeated them in pitched battle time after time. With his son, Jonathan, Saul drove the Philistines out of Israel's lands. For many years his home was a tent on the field of battle and his life a constant round of war and bloodshed.

To soothe his savage moods and drive away the evil spirits that often overcame him, a handsome shepherd named David was brought to Saul to play the harp and sing to the king so that he might be calmed and the evil spirit be driven away.

With the passing of time, David became a great hero of the people. Saul, jealous and afraid, tried to kill the shepherd slayer of Goliath, but each time David escaped. And, as Saul's moods became angrier and his acts wilder, his officers and soldiers began to leave him. His power crumbled slowly. The Philistines, scenting victory, attacked him with renewed ferocity on the plains of Jezreel.

When the battle was over, the Israelites had been routed and Saul and three of his sons lay dead on the battlefield. Thus ended the rule of Saul, first King of Israel. David took his place, but not before singing the generous praise of Saul the warrior and lamenting his death. David sang, "How are the mighty fallen in the midst of the battle!"

SOLOMON

The World's Wisest Man

Solomon, the son of David and Bathsheba, was the third King of Israel. He was, by contrast with the kings before him, a man of peace who built his nation into a great and unified whole through diplomacy and wise leadership.

No man before him had ever been as wise as Solomon. So wise was he that his wisdom became renowned throughout the civilized world, and it has come down to us in the phrase, to be as wise as Solomon. Of the many wise acts attributed to him, none comes more readily to mind than the story of the two women who claimed to be the mother of the same child. Brought before Solomon for judgment, the King of Israel ordered that the child be divided in two by the sword, and one-half given to each woman. When one woman protested bitterly and asked that the child's life be spared and that it be given to the other woman, Solomon declared that only the real mother could be so concerned for the child's life and awarded the baby to her as her own.

Under Solomon's wise rule, the land of Israel grew strong. The wealth of the nation grew greatly, and Solomon drew on the cultures and skills of all the world to make a better life for his people. He built a great and magnificent Temple for them. From all over the world kings and queens came to his resplendent court to sit at his feet and learn from him.

With all his wealth and splendor, his wisdom and devotion to the Lord, Solomon was an arrogant man and harsh with his people. He levied heavy taxes on them and forced them to labor for him. He loved pleasure and extravagance more than was good for him or his people. Eventually, there rose murmurs of rebellion. His power waned as disaffection set in. Upon his death, the kingdom weakened and broke up.

To Solomon are ascribed a number of writings in the Bible, particularly many psalms, proverbs, the Book of Ecclesiastes, and the Song of Songs. For these, for his great wisdom and for the building of the first Temple which, though destroyed, has been a source of inspiration to Jews the world over, Solomon is gratefully remembered.

Baruch
SPINOZA

A Philosopher For The Ages

Baruch Spinoza was one of the greatest philosophers who ever lived, certainly the greatest ever produced by the Jewish people. His life was a tragedy of misunderstanding. As a boy, he studied in Amsterdam in the school of Rabbi Morteira. For nine hours a day, the boy pored over Hebrew, the Talmud and the Jewish philosophers. He was a favorite of the Rabbi and a great future was anticipated for him.

But Spinoza's interests ranged wide over all the fields of learning. He studied mathematics, astronomy, physics. And certain doubts began to plague his mind. When word of Spinoza's heresies came to the ears of the leaders of the Jewish community in Amsterdam, Spinoza was summoned before them. To them, Spinoza declared that God was too great to have revealed Himself to only one people and only in one Law. He held that truth was larger than synagogue or church.

The council of rabbis and learned men excommunicated Spinoza and the proclaimed heretic was driven away from his own people, never again to have relations with them. Alone and ostracised, he lived by himself, making a bare pittance as a grinder of lenses for spectacles. In want and penury, he set to work on the philosophical treatises that were to make for him enduring fame. In 1670, he published a magnificent plea for liberty of thought. All it brought him was condemnation from pulpit and press.

His reputation as the greatest philosopher of his time grew and spread. Ill with a lingering tuberculosis, he spent the last years of his life laboring on his great work, "Ethics." He died at the age of 45, and his great work was not published till after his death. The heart of his heresy and the cause of his ostracism can best be expressed by the answer he once gave a woman who asked him whether Judaism was the best religion because he, a Jew, was such a good man.

"All religions are good," replied Spinoza, "that lead one to a good life."

David Bernard STEINMAN

The Bridge Builder

Born in the shadow of the Brooklyn Bridge in 1886, David Steinman grew up with a great thirst for knowledge. At 13, he was a student in New York's City College. He graduated with the highest honors and three scholarships which enabled him to continue his studies at Columbia where he won a degree in civil engineering as well as his Ph.D. While taking courses, he taught at City College in the evening.

The paper he wrote for his engineering degree was entitled "The Design of the Henry Hudson Memorial Bridge as a Steel Arch." A quarter-century later, Steinman actually built this bridge, one of the most beautiful in the world. At 24, he went on to the University of Idaho as the youngest professor of civil engineering in the country. And he wrote a classic and basic book on suspension bridges.

In 1914, Steinman began his great work in the design of bridges. He helped build the Hell Gate Arch Bridge over New York's East River that established a new record for length. He designed the Sciotoville Bridge over the Ohio River.

His fame grew, and Steinman found himself being called on by every country in the world. In Brazil, he put up the largest bridge in South America. In California, he built the largest cantilever bridge in the United States, the first designed especially to withstand earthquakes. Then there was the Thousand Island Bridge over the St. Lawrence, the St. Johns Bridge in Oregon. There were beautiful suspension bridges in Siam, Australia, Bolivia, Denmark, Haiti, Spain, Germany, and many, many more, in countries thruout the civilized world.

All in all, David Steinman built more than 200 bridges. In his native city of New York, he designed the famous Triborough Bridge, and was consultant on the George Washington Bridge. At the peak of his fame, he was called to the task of remodelling the Brooklyn Bridge, the span in whose shadow he had grown up as a boy.

Many have been the honors, awards, medals and degrees showered on David Steinman, world's greatest living bridge-builder. But in 1956 he worked on, oblivious to them all, creating what will some day be the longest bridge in the world, the great bridge that will span New York Bay from Staten Island to the Brooklyn shore.

Charles P. STEINMETZ

The Giant Dwarf

Charles Steinmetz was a grotesque little man barely four feet tall with enormous head, small dark eyes, and a hump on his back, but his service to science benefited in a practical way all the people of America and the world. Born in Breslau, Germany, in a family which had a long history of inherited deformity, Steinmetz proved to be a brilliant student with a fine mind. Because he engaged in political activity, he was obliged to flee Germany. He came to America when he was 24, learned English in a year, and became a citizen. His first job brought him $12 a week as a draftsman. From then on his career was meteoric.

In five years, Steinmetz was head of General Electric's vital calculating department. Almost immediately, he solved three of the most baffling problems that had hindered electrical progress. His salary soared to $100,000 a year.

The discoveries made by the deformed little man were innumerable. He developed a way to transmit electrical power at high pres-sure without damage. He invented various motors and worked out the modern method of substations for generating plants to furnish power. He made possible cheap car lighting, quick elevator service and modern street lighting. There were many, many more things Steinmetz accomplished for General Electric and the country as a whole.

Perhaps he is best remembered as the modern Jove who could at will produce great lightning bolts in his own laboratory. With what he learned about lightning, Steinmetz was able to show how better to control natural lightning to protect homes and buildings.

Steinmetz never married and died at the age of 58. He was still working in his laboratory, discovering, experimenting, learning. His service to electrical science was not only incalculable, but the full extent of his contributions has not even yet been entirely explored. Steinmetz changed electrical science from a plaything and a curiosity to a powerful tool that could be harnessed and controlled by man for the betterment of his life.

LEVI STRAUSS

A Forty-Niner To Remember

Among the many adventurous men who went to California over a century ago in the feverish hunt for gold was young Levi Strauss. Just 21 years of age, and only one year in America, Strauss had no money to buy the equipment he needed to join the search for the yellow metal. Instead, he brought with him a bundle of fabrics which he hoped to sell for tent covers and wagon tops.

But the miners didn't want cloth for their tents and wagons. They were sorely in need of clothes, especially pants tough enough to withstand rough treatment.

Levi Strauss went to a tailor and had pants made of the heavy canvas he had brought with him from the East. Thus were born, over a hundred years ago, the famous "Levis" that have since become standard wearing apparel of miners and cowboys. In fact, levis eventually became so popular that young people everywhere began to wear them too. There is hardly a youngster who never wore a pair of "Levis." From that beginning, Levi Strauss prospered. He persuaded his brothers in New York to send him more and more material for the levis so much in demand. By the time he was 25, the

Bavarian-born youth had founded the very first —and largest—clothing manufacturing business west of the Mississippi River.

Levi Strauss, who lived to be 72, came to be one of the most beloved characters in the West. So renowned was he for personal honesty and integrity that a common saying heard on all sides was, "You can buy levis for one dollar but you can't buy Levi for a million."

He became wealthy as well as honored, and did much to help bring the first transcontinental railroad to California. He was a devoted member of Temple Emanu-El in San Francisco, remaining faithful to Jewish traditions and observances all his life. Many were his benefactions, not only to his religion, but also to the cause of education and recreation. He set up 28 scholarships at the University of California. They are being offered to this very day.

Famous all through the West as "the cowboys' tailor," Levi Strauss will never be forgotten as long as there are horses to ride or mines to be dug. The useful garment he invented is a memorial to one of the best loved men of the old West. Always he should be remembered as the man who gave America a pair of pants to wear.

NATHAN
STRAUSS

The Savior Of Children

Many a person living today owes his life to the stubbornness and devotion of Nathan Strauss, one of mankind's greatest benefactors. It was thanks to him that the importance of the pasteurization of milk was impressed on people all over the world.

Born in Bavaria, Nathan Strauss was brought to this country as a child. He came to New York from the South when he was 14. Beginning as a bookkeeper, he worked his way up in department store work until he was one of the wealthiest merchants in the world. He took a keen interest in the welfare of his workers and their children. And from that interest, Strauss learned something that was to affect the rest of his life and that of mankind.

Visiting a slum area for the first time, Strauss was appalled to learn how many children died in their early years. He investigated closely the reason for this infant mortality. Soon he became convinced that impure milk was the main cause of fatality in children. Having heard of the work of Louis Pasteur, Strauss went to France to look into it. He returned to America determined to educate the country in the advantages of purifying milk by pasteurization.

He began by setting up pasteurization stations where milk could be treated and sold at cost or less to the poor. For eight long years, he withstood the attacks and ridicule of those who sold milk and did not believe in the process he had installed.

But the results of Strauss's work soon became evident. The death rate fell swiftly among the children. Pasteurization of milk became the accepted standard.

Strauss went on to do many, many more things for the children and the needy. He devoted all his time to philanthropy. Late in life, Strauss, always a devout Jew, went to Palestine where he gave a third of his fortune to setting up milk stations, hospitals, schools and factories. He lived to 83, and every day of his life was a day for giving to the young, the needy and the helpless. To no one more than Nathan Strauss do the children of the world owe more gratitude for his generosity and kindness of heart.

[115]

Oscar S.
STRAUSS

First In A President's Cabinet

In the year 1902, when the Jews of Eastern Europe and Russia were suffering some of the most grievous blows ever visited upon them by cruel and oppressive governments, President Theodore Roosevelt announced the appointment of Oscar S. Strauss to be a member of his cabinet as Secretary of Commerce and Labor. "I want to show the world," he said pointedly, "what I think of the Jews in this country."

This act by the aggressive and hard-hitting T.R. was the first time that a Jew had ever been made a member of a President's cabinet.

Strauss was one of the most respected men in America. A lawyer by profession and a merchant by tradition—he was the brother of Nathan and Isidor Strauss and with them as owner of Macy's, he built it into the largest department store in the world. Oscar Strauss was one of the founders of the American Jewish Historical Society. He was also one of the founders of the famous 92nd Street Y.M.H.A. in New York, the oldest existing Jewish community center and the largest.

One of his unique distinctions is that he served in public life under four different presidents. Besides serving under Roosevelt as a cabinet minister, Strauss was United States Minister to Turkey, appointed first by President Cleveland, and subsequently reappointed to that post by Presidents McKinley and Taft. And from 1902 till his death in 1926, Strauss served as one of the United States members of the Permanent Court of Arbitration at The Hague. Wherever he was called on to serve his country, Oscar Strauss did so with distinction and honor.

Henrietta
SZOLD

Servant Of Her People

Born in Baltimore in 1860, Henrietta Szold was the daughter of a rabbi of great erudition. She studied in Baltimore schools and became a teacher prominent in many activities. Her first connection with the work of organized Jewry came when she became editorial secretary of the Jewish Publication Society and translated a number of Hebrew books, including Graetz's monumental "History of the Jews," and Lazarus' "Ethics of Judaism."

It was in 1898 that Miss Szold organized the first class in Americanization for Jewish immigrants. She rented a room over a store and began this historic work with a class of 30 eager and bewildered pupils recently arrived in the New World.

But it was with her work in Zionism that the name of Henrietta Szold will forever be linked. Her first Zionist speech was made in 1895, and she made her first visit to Palestine in 1909. There she saw for the first time the appalling prevalence of trachoma, dread eye disease that led to so much blindness among children and adults. Determined to do something about the health of the people in the Holy Land, she conceived the idea of district nursing. She organized the American Zionist medical unit which eventually led to the founding by her of Hadassah, the women's Zionist organization.

The small frail-looking woman was a tower of strength to the Jewish people and a dedicated worker for Zionism. At the age of 75, she took arms against the Hitler persecutions as director of Youth Aliyah, the movement which did so much to rescue Jewish children from the Nazi terror and bring them to Palestine.

Henrietta Szold died in Palestine on February 13, 1945. Many memorials exist to honor this great woman who dedicated 65 years of her life to helping her fellow-Jews. But no memorial of stone, no colony named for her, no streets bearing her name, is more real or will endure longer in the minds of world Jewry than her devoted and unselfish work for Zionism and the Jewish homeland.

Dr. Edward TELLER

Father of the Hydrogen Bomb

On November 1, 1952, a new bomb was exploded near a small Pacific island by a United States military force. A little later, President Eisenhower announced that the new bomb had detonated with 25 times the force of the atom bomb. Thus the world learned that the most powerful explosive ever created by man was now in existence. It was the Hydrogen Bomb and its creator and chief architect was a man named Edward Teller.

Born in Budapest, Hungary, in 1908, Edward Teller was the son of well-to-do parents. Even as a boy he showed remarkable aptitude for mathematics. After earning his degree in chemical engineering in 1928 at the Institute of Technology in Budapest, he went on to Munich for further study, specializing in physical chemistry.

In the same year, when he was 20, Teller lost his right foot in a street accident. Despite this handicap, he continued his studies, receiving his Ph.D. at Leipzig where he became research associate in physical chemistry. When he won a Rockefeller fellowship in 1934, he went to Copenhagen to study under Nobel-Prize-winner Niels Bohr, the famous Danish Jew who was one of the world's greatest scientists. When the Nazis seized power, Teller fled to England, then America.

In the United States, Teller became professor of molecular and atomic physics at George Washington University. He continued this work at Columbia University in New York. As one of the earliest proponents of the atomic bomb, Dr. Teller was one of the six scientists who persuaded Albert Einstein to write his now famous letter to President Roosevelt urging the establishment of a development program for the atomic bomb.

After World War II, Dr. Teller became professor of physics at the University of Chicago. Convinced that a more powerful bomb than the A-bomb could be made, he insisted on going on with research in spite of a great deal of opposition. A new laboratory was established for him in California at a cost of $11,500,000. The vindication of his faith in a more powerful bomb came with the making of the world's most destructive weapon, the H-bomb. Because of his fierce dedication to the possibilities of this thermonuclear weapon, Dr. Edward Teller has well earned the title of "Chief Architect of the H-Bomb."

Judah TOURO

America's First Philanthropist

On a tombstone in a cemetery in Newport, Rhode Island, there is an inscription which reads:

By righteousness and integrity he collected his wealth.
In charity and for salvation he dispensed it.
The last of his name, he inscribed it in the Book of philanthropy to be remembered forever.

The grave is that of Judah Touro, the Israelite of New Orleans, who was the first Jewish philanthropist in America. Touro, at the age of 23, left Boston where he had lost a job because he had fallen in love with the owner's daughter, and came to New Orleans to make his fortune. He opened a tiny store near the levee where he sold candles, codfish and soap. Every ship that came to New Orleans from Boston brought him more and more articles for sale in the growing city. Touro grew wealthy, owning great areas of real estate as well as his prospering business.

When the War of 1812 broke out, Touro joined General Andrew Jackson in the great and historic battle for the defense of the city. He was wounded and walked with a limp the rest of his life.

Although he grew richer and richer, Touro did not hoard his wealth but generously gave it away to many causes. When a church fell deeply in debt and bankrupt, Touro bought it at auction for $20,000 and returned it to the minister to continue with God's work. He founded the great hospital in the city which bears his name. He made the largest contribution to the fund for the erection of Bunker Hill Monument. He helped the Jews build synagogues and built a home for orphan boys. And he founded the very first free library in the city of New Orleans.

A single man with no family, Touro wanted to continue to serve all mankind even after his death. To every synagogue in existence at the time in America, to every Hebrew school, hospital and relief society, he left a share of his great fortune. He even left a fund for the care of the street on which the ancient Newport Synagogue stands. Judah Touro died as he had lived, a simple unassuming man. But the good he did so many years ago guarantees that his name will indeed "be remembered forever."

Selman Abraham WAKSMAN

Discoverer Of A Wonder Drug

Selman Waksman was quietly doing research in his chosen field of microbiology at Rutgers University in 1941. His salary was a meager $4,620 a year. A university official, checking the budget of the school, came across the name of Waksman and saw little either in his work or his prospects to warrant further experiment or research. He urged that Waksman be let go as a waste of time and money.

The university authorities refused to fire Waksman, much to their credit. And a little later, there came from that research one of the great boons of medicine, the antibiotic streptomycin, called by the grateful world the "wonder drug."

Born in the village of Priluka, Russia, in 1888, Selman Waksman had been urged to study industrial chemistry. He came to America in 1910 and, instead, entered the Rutgers College of Agriculture to study microbiology. After graduating in 1915, he went on to take his Ph.D. at California. He returned to Rutgers to teach and do research.

For 28 years Waksman pored over his test tubes in the little laboratory on the Rutgers campus. It was his theory that there were in the soil microorganisms which would prove beneficial to mankind, and that there were more different living things under the surface of the earth than on it.

Success crowned his efforts at last when Waksman announced the discovery of his wonder drug. With it there came into existence a substance that was to save millions of lives from diseases that had long baffled science. At the same time, Waksman achieved worldwide fame. Honors poured in on him from all quarters of the globe. In 1952, he was awarded the coveted Nobel Prize in medicine.

Waksman signed over all rights to the earnings from his wonder drug to Rutgers and his salary was raised to $10,000 plus 10% of the royalties. Streptomycin has paid for further research and many new buildings for the university, including a new laboratory for himself. A steady stream of new discoveries, new antibiotics like actinomycin, neomycin, clavacin and many others, have issued from that laboratory. The world forever must be grateful to the fertile mind of the discoverer of antibiotics.

Lillian
WALD

An Angel Of The Slums

Though she had been reared in luxury, Lillian Wald chose to throw in her lot with the under-privileged rather than pursue the social life that was open to her. She studied nursing in a New York city hospital, then moved to the East Side where poverty and disease were grinding down the poor. She ran classes to teach the immigrants how to take care of their health. One day, when a child came to her as she was teaching and told her that her mother was dying, Lillian Wald left her class and went with the little girl to see the sick woman. Thus she began the first visiting nurse service in history. And 50 years later, there were more than 20,000 such visiting nurses in the United States.

Miss Wald soon moved to larger quarters on Henry Street so she could have room for all who came to see her for help. So was founded the famous Henry Street Settlement, best known institution of its kind in the world. In the back yard, she set up a sort of park where young and old could play and rest. That became the first playground in the country. Because of it, in time, cities all over the land established other playgrounds.

Meanwhile, Lillian Wald was carrying on a running feud with politicians for better housing, for protection of the children, for the elimination of social evils. Little by little, her pressure brought results. In 1908, a federal Children's Bureau was set up. Before that, she had organized the first city school nursing service, a model for what was to become regular medical care for school children. And she was the first to start bedside schooling for the handicapped youngsters.

Lillian Wald died in 1940, but not before she was able to see how rich were the fruits of her labors. Known during her lifetime as "The Angel of Henry Street," Lillian Wald was visited by a procession of Presidents, ministers, famous men and women from all over the world who came to see what she was accomplishing. They talked and listened to her with respect and admiration. But the children whose very lives they owed to her could hardly believe that she was responsible for it all. In their direct and simple way they said to whoever asked, "God must live in the Henry Street Settlement."

David
WARFIELD

The World's Richest Actor

Of the many actors of Jewish extraction who have won fame and fortune on the American stage, the first to win national acclaim was David Warfield. Like many others who went on to recognition in the legitimate theatre, Warfield had his start on the burlesque stage. Born in California in 1866, Warfield, then David Wollfeld, got his first job as a boy selling programs in a San Francisco theatre. He soon rose to usher and began to think of getting on the stage itself. He was quite talented as a mimic and teller of funny stories. His chance came when he was hired by a music hall. The experience was devastating. Warfield was hissed off by a howling audience.

Undiscouraged by this hostile reception, Warfield went to New York. For a time he starved and scraped, paying $1.50 a week for a shabby hotel room and subsisting on a couple of rolls a day for food. At last, in 1895, he joined the celebrated Weber and Fields burlesque company as a Jewish comic, presenting funny but lovable characters on the stage.

One day, David Belasco saw Warfield in burlesque and offered him a chance to work in the legitimate theatre. Theatre-wise people hooted at the idea of a burlesque clown becoming a dramatic actor. But Belasco was not a theatre genius for nothing. He cast Warfield in a play and, in a short time, the former burlesque star was holding Broadway audiences in the palm of his hand. His fame grew and even spanned the Atlantic. As star of "The Music Master," he earned over $300,000 for a single season's work. Hollywood offered him a million dollars in cold cash to make a single picture. He refused, for he had become the world's wealthiest actor and money was no longer any inducement to him.

In 1922, Warfield performed the role of Shylock in Shakespeare's "Merchant of Venice" and his novel interpretation of the role created a great controversy. Angered by the dispute over his portrayal, the 58-year-old Warfield quit the stage forever. He left behind him a rich gallery of great roles but more than that, he retired from the theatre with a fortune estimated at over $12,000,000. He lived till he was 80, a living legend of the American theatre.

CHAIM WEIZMANN

First President Of Israel

"It doesn't matter how small your home is, it only matters that you should have a place called home." So said Chaim Weizmann once, and he gave fifty years of his life to the struggle for a place that could be called home by the Jewish people.

Born in a ghetto town in Poland, Weizmann studied in Germany and Switzerland and took his degree in chemistry. Always an ardent Zionist, he came to England to pursue his career. When World I broke out, he flung himself into chemical research, for England was desperately in need of help in the fight. In 1915, Weizmann discovered a vitally needed process for making acetone, basic in the production of explosives. A grateful British government sought to reward the brilliant chemist. But Weizmann refused all honors for himself. His dream of a Jewish homeland was still uppermost in his mind. "Do something for my people," he said. "I want nothing for myself."

Two years later, in 1917, Weizmann received the reward he sought. England issued the famous Balfour Declaration, opening Palestine to Jewish settlement. A homeland had at last been found!

Weizmann practically gave up his career as a chemist to throw himself into the struggle for the reconstruction of the barren land of Palestine. For 25 years, as President of the World Zionist Organization, he travelled to all parts of the world to raise funds for the task of rebuilding and to interest every person he could reach in the project. And, as the new land grew in population and flourished in industry and agriculture, Weizmann pressed on to found famed Hebrew University in Jerusalem and the Weizmann Institute of Science.

More than three decades were to pass before the Balfour Declaration wrung from Britain bore fruit at last in the establishment of Israel as a free and independent nation. On May 16, 1948, Israel came into existence, and Chaim Weizmann, now ill, weary and nearly blind, was elected the first President of the new nation. He lived only four years longer. Scientist, statesman, educator and political zealot, the Moses of the 20th century left behind him a monument to mark his place in history, a place that could truly be called home by the Jews of the world—Israel!

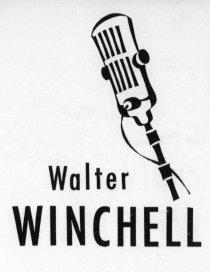

Walter
WINCHELL

Father Of The Gossip Column

For good or for bad, admired or despised, Walter Winchell has proved himself the most controversial newspaper reporter in the world. Originator of a new form of journalism, the gossip column, the dynamic Winchell has revitalized news reporting so that for 25 years, more than 30 million people have read his newspaper column, daily, and more than 25 million people have listened to his once-a-week radio broadcasts.

Walter Winchell was born in 1897, the son of Jewish immigrant parents. He grew up in a dingy New York City tenement. He had a bitter boyhood. The family was poor, and Walter often found himself taken care of by strangers when food and money ran out at home. He often played hookey from school so he could work as a candy hawker in a local theatre. Because of this, he was still in the sixth grade when he was 13. A year later, he left school forever, and joined the famous Gus Edwards Revue. He toured the country with that troupe of child stage performers, all destined for eventual fame.

In 1919, Winchell struck out on his own as a vaudeville actor with a song-and-dance routine. While hoofing, he amused himself by writing a gossip column strictly for the stage people he worked with, and posting it each week on bulletin boards backstage. It became popular with the actors. Eventually, Winchell's gossip column was printed in a vaudeville magazine, and his pay for writing it was $25 a week. Soon, it was being printed in a daily newspaper in New York.

Winchell became an indefatigable hunter of sensational and spicy news for his Broadway column. The personal lives of the famous became grist for his mill. His gossip column became so popular that before long, it was being syndicated in 800 newspapers, and this man who never had passed the sixth grade of a public school, became the highest paid writer in the history of journalism. His income soared to more than $10,000 a week.

In 1932, Winchell also became a radio news commentator. And the fabulous originator of modern-day gossip columning became a sensation for the second time. Millions listened to him. He expanded his scope as a gossip columnist, and plunged into politics. He championed many causes. Courageously, he criticized the activities of United States Senators, Congressmen, Governors, and politicians when he believed that they had outstepped the bounds of decency and righteousness. He even took to task Presidents of the United States and world leaders. He began to influence national and foreign policies, and he became a vigorous national figure to be reckoned with in the flow of American social and political life.

So he has remained something of a legend on the American scene, and for more than 25 years, he has remained the most controversial newspaper reporter of this or any other century.

Rabbi Isaac Mayer WISE

Architect Of The Jewish Reformation

When the thousands of Jews who came to America as immigrants made contact with the vigorous freedom of their new surroundings, it was inevitable that there should be important changes not only in their lives but also in their manner of worship. It was Isaac Mayer Wise who acted as the architect of this change which can be called the Jewish Reformation. To Wise much of the custom and ceremonial of Jewish ritual were obsolete and out of place in the New World. He devoted his life to making Jewish worship fit the American way of life.

Born in Bohemia in 1819, he was the son of a poor *melamed* who earned barely enough to support his brood. At the age of 4, Isaac was already a pupil studying the Talmud in his father's *cheder*. Determined to become a rabbi, he went on to study in the famous rabbinical schools of Prague and Vienna. A full-fledged rabbi at 23, he soon set sail for America where, after a stormy 63-day voyage, he settled in New York for a while, teaching other immigrants for his daily bread. After a short stay as rabbi at Albany, New York, he was hired by the Bene Jeshurun congregation in Cincinnati. There he remained for the next 50 years, changing, altering and revising ritual and custom until they took on the form they have today. An orthodox synagogue to begin with, Bene Jeshurun became a reform congregation. Rabbi Wise installed a mixed choir. He put in an organ. He introduced the idea of worship without covering the head. He instituted Friday night services for the first time in America. He introduced family pews so that men and women could worship together.

Meanwhile he was agitating for a uniform system for all Hebrew schools. In 1855, he opened the first school for rabbis in this country which was to become Hebrew Union College. To establish this school firmly, Rabbi Wise had first to organize the Union of American Hebrew Congregations. In 1874, Rabbi Wise was made president of the college he had fought so hard to get. When he was 71, he formed the last of the three great organizations he founded, the Central Conference of American Rabbis. When he died, in 1900, Rabbi Wise could feel justified in all that he had done, for 61 graduates of his Hebrew Union College were the rabbis of the leading Jewish reform congregations in America.

[125]

Eliezer Ben YEHUDAH

He Revived A Language

Born Eliezer Perlman in Vilna, Lithuania, in 1858, Eliezer Ben Yehudah settled in Palestine in 1881. From that year to his death in 1922, he devoted his life to the study of Hebrew and to its revival as living every-day speech. Thanks to him, Hebrew is today the official language of Israel, living and vibrant.

In the beginning, there were many protests against Yehudah's attempt to make the words of prayer and devotion into the language of the streets. Not only the Yiddish-speaking common people who found it difficult and strange but also the scholars and teachers who held Hebrew to be sacred resisted Yehudah's campaign. But he was stubborn and determined to have his way. He himself spoke no other tongue but Hebrew, although he was versed in many. Even his own wife was not allowed to address him in any other tongue. To further his idea, Yehudah set to work to compile a modern Hebrew dictionary of vast scope. He arranged Hebrew words, both old and modern, in ac-

cordance with the principles of scientific philology of which he was a master, and created new words, new expressions, and new terms where they were needed for ordinary use.

His refusal to speak any other language but Hebrew, his fanatical insistence that others speak it to him, made Yehudah a symbol of Jewish determination to make a new life in the Holy Land. Slowly the ridicule and derision stopped as the ancient tongue in modern form found grudging acceptance. Soon his stubbornness won out completely. Hebrew was reborn as a living tongue and became the language of Israel.

Yehudah became the accepted authority on Hebrew as a spoken language. Thanks to him and his courage, Hebrew, the language of the prophets and the Talmud, has become not only a language of great beauty but also the living speech of a people, equal to any in the civilized world. The Hebrew dictionary, compiled after years of work and devotion has been left by Eliezer Ben Yehudah as a precious legacy to the Jewish people.

Adolph ZUKOR

Pioneer With A Magic Lantern

One of the true pioneers of the moving picture industry, Adolph Zukor was born in Hungary in 1873. His father was a storekeeper, his mother the daughter of a rabbi. But Zukor hardly got to know them. He was an orphan at 8 and went to live with his uncle who was also a rabbi.

By the time he was 14, Zukor had heard a thousand glowing tales of that fabulous land, America. In 1888, at 15, he took the great step. When he landed on the shores of the new land, he had $40 and a burning ambition to make his way in the world.

By the time he was 19, Zukor had made a great success—as a furrier. Then he grew restless and looked about him for something more exciting to do. His eye fell on the penny arcade and nickelodeon business. They fascinated him. So, in 1903, Adolph Zukor took most of his savings and opened a penny arcade on New York's 14th Street.

The penny arcade was a grand success. Zukor opened others in Philadelphia and Boston. The fur business was left far behind as he saw a brilliant future in the flickering pictures that were exciting everybody. Soon he converted the nickelodeon into a straight moving picture theatre. Eventually, he was to be the first man to build a theatre in America devoted exclusively to motion pictures.

By the time he was 40, Zukor had proved himself to be a great showman and the most successful film producer in the fast-growing movie industry. First to pay huge salaries to leading movie actors, Zukor also broke ground in the film business when he first signed a great stage star for a feature picture. This was none other than the famous French-Jewish actress, Sarah Bernhardt, who played the lead for Zukor in a multiple-reel feature called "Queen Elizabeth."

During his 50 years in show business, Zukor brought to the screen many unknowns who were to become the world's greatest stars. He created a sensation when he hired Mary Pickford for $500 a week to work for him. As founder of the Paramount Picture Corporation, Adolph Zukor lived and made history as one of movieland's most honored pioneers.